Pass the Bar Exam!

Three Books in One

Featuring:

Pass the Bar Exam
with Dr. Stipkala's Proven Method

Perspectives on Passing the Bar Exam

Bonus Material: Issue Spotting and
Essay Writing Techniques

Edited by Jeremy M. Stipkala, Ph.D., J.D.

Persimmon Woods Press, LLC

Paperback Book ISBN 978-0-9997997-8-9

Pass the Bar Exam
with Dr. Stipkala's Proven Method
By
Jeremy M. Stipkala, Ph.D., J.D.

Perspectives on Passing the Bar Exam
By
Peter L. Brewer, Esq.
Sabrina C. Call, Esq.
Bernard S. Klosowski, Jr., Esq.
John M. Rappold, Esq., and
Jeremy M. Stipkala, Esq.

Bonus Material:
Issue Spotting and Essay Writing
Techniques
By
Jeremy M. Stipkala, Ph.D., J.D.

Pass the Bar Exam with Dr. Stipkala's Proven Method

By

Jeremy M. Stipkala, Ph.D., J.D.

To Codey, my inspiration, my muse!

Table of Contents

I. Introduction

You have graduated from law school. Congratulations! You should be extremely proud of your achievement. You are joining an honored, noble, and justice-enabling profession. We lawyers are the workers and warriors who build, maintain, and defend the *foundational structure of civilization itself.*

There is just one teeny tiny little problem. You have to pass the bar exam to receive a license to do all that building, maintaining, and defending. And do not forget all the rent paying, grocery buying, and student-loan repaying that you have to do, too. That bar exam is a two or three-day contest in which you must regurgitate *everything* you ever learned in law school. And if you eventually fail to achieve a passing score, *your investment in your law school education will have been for naught.* (I vastly overstate the demands and importance of the bar exam, but you will not believe me until you **pass**.)

There is just one further teeny tiny little problem: Law school does not adequately prepare you to take the bar exam. Sure, law school attempts to teach you the law. Perhaps, law school teaches you how to think like a lawyer. Maybe even more than you care to remember, law school also exposes you to the think-on-your-feet kind of stress that lawyers sometimes endure. *But law school does not teach you how to study for and pass the bar exam!* "Really?" you ask. Yes, really, I answer. When was the last time you braved six hours of examination in a day, two or three days in a row, in a life-changing, make-or-break kind of way?

Consider running a marathon. How would you train for the marathon? You can read books and books about how to train for and run a marathon. You can watch videos, even movies, about others who have conquered the feat (feet?). But do you think that reading all the books and watching all the videos in the world about marathons would allow you to run 26.2 miles with any hope of success, or of even living through it? Dear Reader, it would be foolish and dangerous for you to read a book about running a marathon, and then go strap on some comfortable shoes and take off down the street for 26.2 miles with no other preparation.

Going further with the marathon analogy, law school vis-à-vis the bar exam prepares you to run nice little 5K and 10K fun runs. Surely a person who can run ten kilometers (six miles) is more likely to finish a marathon (alive) than a person who leads a completely sedentary lifestyle. Even so, our hypothetical fun-runner needs to train, and train differently, before she steps up to the starting line on Marathon Day.

That is what this book aims to do. Let's take smart people who have graduated law school, and teach them, *train them,* to pass the bar exam – mentally and physically. That is you, Dear Reader! Graduating from law school **proves** that you can pass the bar exam. That was a marathon of a different sort; now we will train for a new marathon since you have proven that you can run well.

Your mentor's credentials are ample. I have studied for, taken, and passed the bar exams in South Carolina, Virginia, and Washington, D.C., in addition to the United States Patent Bar Exam. In the course of those victories, I have honed my approach into a tested – *and proven* – method for passing any bar exam. I have mentored friends who have not passed the bar exam, and seen them adopt my successful method to turn discouraging failure into **magnificent triumph**. My hard-fought and hard-won achievements on those bar exams and with those friends burn inside of me, and I strongly desire to pass on what I have learned so that you, Dear Reader, can get your license to practice law sooner rather than later. If I help you to pass the bar exam, remember to pay it forward: Help some future law school graduate study for, *train for,* and pass the bar exam.

II. How to Study

A. Planning Your Study

How do you study, train, *prepare* for a bar exam? There are three essential aspects to your bar exam preparation. First, you need to internalize a considerable amount of substantive law. Second, you have got to practice, practice, practice. (If this were a marathon, you would have to run, run, run.) Third, you must manage the precious time you have to prepare. The bar exam will happen at the end of February, or at the end of July, whether you are ready or not.

Let us see how those three essential aspects combine in a suitable preparation plan. Suppose it is January 1st or June 1st, and you will take the bar exam on the last Tuesday and Wednesday in February or July. That gives you approximately fifty days to study. If at all possible, clear your schedule of every other responsibility. Take a leave of absence from your job; send your kids to grandma's for two months. If it is not possible for you to do those things, then may God bless you. You can still pass the bar exam, but it will be more demanding. (I have seen people do it – pass the bar exam while working *and* taking care of kids!) Simply put, your plan should give adequate attention to each subject, both to absorb and to practice, given the time. If you have to choose between studying and practicing, *choose practicing.* You may face a question for which you do not remember or have not studied the law no matter how much you study; later chapters will explore how to successfully attack that question. For now, know that tackling *practice test questions* will hone those skills.

First, you must determine the areas of substantive law that will appear on your bar exam. Your state bar website should list subjects that will be tested. Also, your law school will have information about the bar exam for the state where the school is. Many states (twenty-eight at the time of this writing) use the Uniform Bar Examination created by the National Conference of Bar Examiners. It is imperative that you learn early which subjects will be tested on your bar exam, so that you don't have a nasty surprise on Exam Day. These are the subjects tested by the essay portion of the Uniform Bar Examination:

Business Associations
Civil Procedure
Conflict of Laws
Constitutional Law
Contracts and Article 2 of the UCC
Criminal Law and Procedure
Evidence
Family Law
Real Property
Secured Transactions and Article 9 of the UCC
Torts
Trusts and Estates

FIND OUT **ALL** OF THE SUBJECTS BEING TESTED IN YOUR JURISDICTION *BEFORE* CRAFTING YOUR STUDY PLAN! You don't want to miss studying a tested subject, obviously.

These are the subjects tested by the multiple-choice portion of the Uniform Bar Examination:

Civil Procedure
Constitutional Law
Contracts and Articles 1 and 2 of the UCC
Criminal Law and Procedure
Evidence
Real Property
Torts

Then, of course, there is **the practical test**. Let us treat the practical test as equal to an essay subject as we develop our study plan.

(If you will take the Puerto Rico bar, then *vaya con Dios*. Louisiana bar? *Laissez les bons temps rouler!* I have no personal experience with those bar exams. However, I believe I have something useful in here for you nonetheless.)

Now that you know the substantive areas of the law that you have to internalize, make a calendar that manages internalization, practice, and time. For each day, list those subjects and tasks that you will perform. If you are studying for the bar exam without benefit of a commercial program that schedules your preparation for you, your calendar might look like this:

Day 1: TORTS. Morning: Study torts for internalization (more on how to study for internalization below). Torts are "fun" and engaging, and you probably had some idea about torts even before you went to law school. That makes torts a good place to start! Afternoon: Do a torts practice essay. Look up the law after you read the fact pattern, and keep the chapter on "Essays" below handy. Then write the essay in full. Note how long it takes. Do ten practice multiple-choice questions on torts. Look up the correct answers immediately. Then continue to study torts. Bonus: Have you made your travel and accommodations arrangements for the bar exam? Have you elected whether to write or type your essays? Attend to those matters as needed.

Day 2: TORTS. Morning: Start with ten multiple-choice questions on torts. This will get your adrenaline flowing. Continue studying torts. Afternoon: Practice essay on torts. Write out the essay in full. Do twenty multiple-choice questions on torts. Continue studying torts.

Day 3: TORTS. Morning: Start with twenty multiple-choice questions on torts. Afternoon: Do a practice essay on torts, and fifty multiple-choice questions on torts. Try hard not to peek at the law or the answers as you tackle those questions. But, once you finish the practice test, look up the model answers for essays and correct answers for multiple-choice questions and study why they are correct. Also look up the relevant black letter law in your source materials and in the study materials (outline, flashcards, whatever) that you are creating. Are your study materials effective? Is the material sticking? Are you able to internalize and then *utilize* the material on the practice questions? Finish torts today. If your elaborate outline on torts suitable for passing on to posterity is not finished yet, you need to simplify or jettison that endeavor. You've got to make your internalization efforts efficient so that you can cover all subjects.

Day 4: CIV PRO. Morning: Study civil procedure. Afternoon: Do twenty multiple-choice questions on civil procedure. Do a practice essay on civil procedure, writing your answer in full. Peek at the law and model answer as needed.

Day 5: CIV PRO. Morning: Study civil procedure. Start with ten multiple-choice questions. Afternoon: Practice essay on civil procedure – just outline your answer. Peek as needed, but try to articulate a rule of law before you peek. Do twenty multiple-choice questions on civil procedure. Continue studying civil procedure.

Day 6: CIV PRO. Morning: Start with twenty multiple-choice questions. Continue studying civil procedure. Afternoon: Outline two essays on civil procedure. Do fifty multiple-choice questions. Finish studying civil procedure.

Day 7: TEST DAY. Write out essays on torts and civil procedure, under realistic test conditions. Do fifty multiple-choice questions each on torts and civil procedure, under realistic test conditions. Immediately check the right answers for the questions you got wrong, and look up the law on each. Find the law in your source materials, and correlate the articulation of the law with the structure of the question. Say "aha!" when you see the connection! Do sets of twenty multiple-choice questions on torts and civil procedure through the afternoon. Shore up any review you need on torts and civil procedure.

Day 8: CRIM PRO. Morning: Study criminal law and procedure. Afternoon: Do twenty multiple-choice questions. Peek at the answers as needed. Immediately look up the correct answers to all questions when you have finished the twenty questions. Outline an essay. Continue studying. (I won't keep repeating suggestions in this list calendar like: Time your practice questions; try not to peek at the answers or the law until you have made an attempt at outlining an answer; when you finish outlining/writing an essay or doing all ten/twenty/fifty multiple-choice questions, look up the answers and the law at least for the questions you missed.)

Day 9: CRIM PRO. Morning: Start with twenty multiple-choice questions. Continue studying. Afternoon: Do twenty multiple-choice questions, and outline an essay. Continue studying.

Day 10: CRIM PRO. Morning: Start with twenty multiple-choice questions. Continue studying. Afternoon: Do fifty multiple-choice questions, and outline two essays. Finish criminal law and procedure today.

Day 11: EVIDENCE. Evidence and criminal law and procedure go well together. Isn't criminal procedure ultimately about presenting evidence? Morning: Study. Afternoon: Do twenty multiple-choice questions. Peek, peek, peek. But guess first! Outline an essay. Peek at the model answer and the law as needed.

Day 12: EVIDENCE. Morning: Start with twenty multiple-choice questions. Continue studying. Afternoon: Outline an essay. Try not to peek. Do twenty multiple-choice questions. Look up the correct answers and the law when you finished with the twenty questions. Continue studying evidence.

Day 13: EVIDENCE. Morning: Start with twenty multiple-choice questions. Continue studying. Afternoon: Do fifty multiple-choice questions. Outline two essay questions on evidence.

Day 14: TEST DAY. Write out full essays, one each, for criminal law and procedure and evidence, under realistic test conditions. Do fifty questions apiece for criminal law and procedure and evidence, under realistic test conditions. Outline essays for torts, civil procedure, criminal law and procedure, and evidence. Can you get the outlines done in about ten minutes? Do sets of twenty multiple-choice questions on each of torts, civil procedure, criminal law and procedure, and evidence – keep doing sets of twenty questions, switching subjects, and looking up answers and law when you are done your twenty questions.

Day 15: CON LAW. Constitutional law goes well after criminal procedure. Morning: Study. Afternoon: Do twenty multiple-choice questions, and outline an essay. Peek freely, but guess at the answer first. Bonus: Is there anything else you need to do to be admitted to the bar exam? Has the bar acknowledged your request to write/type the essays? Have you received your registration paper that will allow you into the bar exam on Exam Day? Is it correct? Attend to those matters as needed.

Day 16: CON LAW. Morning: Do twenty multiple-choice questions, and continue studying. Afternoon: Do twenty multiple-choice questions and outline an essay. Continue studying.

Day 17: CON LAW. Morning: Start with twenty multiple-choice questions, and continue studying. Afternoon: Outline two essays, and do fifty multiple-choice questions. Continue studying.

Day 18: CON LAW. Morning: Start with twenty multiple-choice questions, and continue studying. Afternoon: Outline two essays, and do fifty multiple-choice questions. Finish constitutional law today.

Day 19: TEST DAY. Yes, have a test day after only one more subject. Constitutional law is a little bit complicated, and so bears test-driven review right after. Morning: Do fifty multiple-choice questions on constitutional law, and write out a full practice essay on constitutional law. Afternoon: Do twenty multiple-choice questions in each of torts, civil procedure, evidence, and criminal law and procedure. Do a full essay question in any one of torts, civil procedure, criminal law and procedure, and evidence, and outline an essay question in each of the remaining subjects. (That is, if you wrote an essay in torts, outline essays in civil procedure, criminal law and procedure, and evidence.)

Day 20: CONTRACTS. Morning: Study contracts law and Articles 1 and 2 of the Uniform Commercial Code (collectively, "contracts"). Afternoon: Do twenty multiple-choice questions, and outline an essay. Peek as needed. Continue studying.

Day 21: CONTRACTS. Morning: Do twenty multiple-choice questions, and continue studying. Afternoon: Do twenty multiple-choice questions and outline an essay. Continue studying.

Day 22: CONTRACTS. Morning: Start with twenty multiple-choice questions, and continue studying. Afternoon: Do fifty multiple-choice questions and outline two essays. Finish contracts today.

Day 23: PROPERTY. Contracts and real property go together well. One relates to personal property, and the other relates to real property. (When will they add **intellectual property** to the bar exam? We patent attorneys can only hope . . .) Morning: Study real property law. Afternoon: Do ten multiple-choice questions. Guess, then peek. Outline an essay, and peek, peek, peek. Continue studying.

Day 24: PROPERTY. Morning: Start with twenty multiple-choice questions. Continue studying. Afternoon: Do twenty multiple-choice questions, and outline an essay. Continue studying.

Day 25: PROPERTY. Morning: Do twenty multiple-choice questions, and continue studying. Afternoon: Do twenty multiple-choice questions, and outline an essay. Continue studying real property.

Day 26: PROPERTY. Morning: Do twenty multiple-choice questions. Continue studying. Afternoon: Do fifty multiple-choice questions, and outline two essays in real property. Finish studying real property today.

Day 27: TEST DAY. Morning: Do fifty multiple-choice questions in contracts, and then fifty multiple-choice questions in real property. Study the correct answers. Afternoon: Do twenty multiple-choice questions in each of torts, civil procedure, criminal law and procedure, evidence, constitutional law, contracts, and real property. After each twenty-question set, study the correct answers. Review the subjects causing you the most difficulty. Get a good night's rest.

Day 28: TEST DAY. Morning: Do a three-hour practice multiple-choice test on all subjects. That's one hundred randomly-arranged questions. Manage your time to get through the exam. Fill in bubbles on an answer sheet with a Number Two pencil. Be sure to mark the answer next to the number of the question you are answering! Make the practice test conditions as realistic as possible – attempt no food, water, or breaks. Afternoon: Study the right answers on the practice test. Look up the law, too. Review the subjects starting with the one you struggled with the most.

Day 29: TEST DAY. Morning: Do a three-and-a-half-hour essay test covering each of torts, civil procedure, criminal law and procedure, evidence, constitutional law, contracts, and real property, allotting thirty minutes to each subject. Make the exam conditions as realistic as possible. Use the same booklets and pens (or laptop) you will use on Exam Day. Yes, three and a half hours is more than you will endure on Exam Day. But we are building callouses here. Feel the burn. I know it sucks. But make it suck here, and it will suck less on Exam Day. Write out all answers in full. What is the quality of your essay answers? How mushy is your brain at the end? Can you read your own handwriting? How is your time management? Feel the grim joy that when you reach thirty minutes, you are done with that question. Build the discipline to move onto the next question no matter what. Battle feelings of panic and discouragement, and know that you are building the skills, knowledge, strength, and stamina to *pass the bar exam and become a real live lawyer!* Afternoon: Study the model answers to the essay questions. Review those subjects that gave you the most difficulty.

Day 30: CATCH-UP DAY. Whew. Use this day to rest, reflect, go for a walk, clear your mind. You are more than halfway ready for the bar exam! Or, if Life has been Happening to you, use this day to realign your study plan. Perhaps you needed an extra day to finish studying a subject, and so this day became your test day for essays. I suspect that you will need this day for making progress, so don't book a vacay.

Day 31: PRACTICAL TEST. Morning: Read a practical test library, peek at the model answer, and outline your response. Keep the chapter below on the practical test handy. Read another practical test library, and outline a response before peeking at the model answer. Afternoon: Do a ninety-minute practical test. How was your time management? What was the quality of your response? How close did you come to the model answer? (Note: You do *not* have to match the model answer!)

Day 32: BUS. ASSOCS. Business associations law has a certain self-consistent logic once you get into the subject. Morning: Study the law of business associations. Afternoon: Outline an essay. Feel free to peek: you are just getting into this subject. Continue studying. Bonus: Do twenty multiple-choice questions that could address all subjects. Take thirty-six minutes to do the questions, and twenty-four minutes to study the answers and the law on the questions you missed. In other words, twenty questions should take you an hour of testing and review. (Take longer on review if you need to.)

Day 33: BUS. ASSOCS. Morning: Outline an essay on business associations. Continue studying. Afternoon: Outline another essay on business associations, and continue studying. Bonus: Do twenty multiple-choice questions on random subjects.

Day 34: BUS. ASSOCS. Morning: Outline an essay to get started. Continue studying. Afternoon: Outline an essay, and then write a full essay. Finish studying business associations. Bonus: Do twenty multiple-choice questions on random subjects.

Day 35: SEC. TRANS. Secured transactions kind of goes with business associations, right? Morning: Study the law of secured transactions and Article 9 of the Uniform Commercial Code (together, "secured transactions"). Afternoon: Outline an essay. Peek if you must. Continue studying secured transactions. Bonus: Do twenty multiple-choice questions on random subjects.

Day 36: SEC. TRANS. Morning: Outline an essay. Continue studying. Afternoon: Outline another essay, then continue studying. Bonus: Do twenty multiple-choice questions on random subjects.

Day 37: SEC. TRANS. Morning: Outline an essay, and continue studying. Afternoon: Outline an essay, and then finish studying secured transactions. Bonus: Do twenty multiple-choice questions on random subjects.

Day 38: TEST DAY. Write a full essay on business associations, and a full essay on secured transactions, under realistic test conditions. Outline essay questions on each subject studied so far. Outlining should take ten minutes per question, or certainly no more than fifteen. Do fifty multiple-choice questions under realistic test conditions.

Day 39: FAMILY. Ah, family law. In real life, family law lawyers encounter humanity at its worst. Perhaps it should be called un-family law. But the horror is mitigated by at least one rule. We lawyers step in to find and enforce "the best interest of the child." That gives courts leeway to help people in distressful circumstances do The Right Thing for their kids. But I digress. Morning: Study un-family law. Start with marriage, the romantic side of family law, if you can. Afternoon: Outline an essay in family law. Continue studying. Bonus: Do twenty multiple-choice questions on random subjects.

Day 40: FAMILY. Morning: Outline an essay, and continue studying. Afternoon: Outline an essay, and continue studying family law. Bonus: Do twenty multiple-choice questions on random subjects.

Day 41: FAMILY. Morning: Outline an essay. Continue studying. Afternoon: Outline two essays, and finish family law today. (Are you a pro at internalizing and utilizing the knowledge of a subject yet?)

(I'm not saying that you should feel like God's gift to *e.g.,* family law right now, but hopefully your internalization and especially your growing ability to tackle questions should give you confidence that you are progressing *to pass the bar exam.*) Bonus: Do twenty multiple-choice questions on random subjects.

Day 42: TRUSTS & ESTATES. Trusts and estates law follows family law well, I think. Keep it all in the family, right? Morning: Study the law of Dead People and Their Stuff. Afternoon: Outline an essay, and continue studying. Bonus: Do twenty multiple-choice questions on random subjects.

Day 43: TRUSTS & ESTATES. Morning: Outline an essay, and then study. Afternoon: Outline two essays, and continue studying. (Do you see yet what I am doing? By having you tackle questions early, I hope to accomplish at least two things. First, the structure of the questions inspires and directs your studying. Second, by looking at questions before you have internalized the entire subject, and doing that over and over as you begin each new subject, you dispel feelings of panic when you encounter a question on an area of law you have not studied, or momentarily feel you have forgotten. You are training your brain to respond effectively when you face a question asking for seemingly unknown law.) Bonus: Do twenty multiple-choice questions on random subjects.

Day 44: TRUSTS & ESTATES. Morning: Outline an essay, and then study. Afternoon: Outline two essays, and finish trusts and estates. Bonus: Do twenty multiple-choice questions on random subjects.

Day 45: TEST DAY. Write out two full essays, one apiece in family law and trusts and estates. Outline essays in each subject studied so far. Look up the model answers and law for each essay, both the ones you wrote in full and the ones you outlined. Do one hundred multiple-choice questions that cover every subject. (Yes, that should take three hours.) Look up the correct answers and the law governing them. (By now, that should go without saying.)

Day 46: CONFLICTS. It is rare, in my view, to have a full-on essay just about conflicts of laws. Conflicts could appear in family law, trusts and estates law, and sometimes civil procedure and criminal procedure questions. Something happens in one state, and then people re-domicile, die, or flee to another state. So here is conflicts of laws at the end. Morning: Study conflicts of laws. Afternoon: Outline an essay on conflicts. (If you can't find any, make up a question. Decedent made a will in State A, has stuff in States A & B, owes money to someone in State C. Where should we probate the will?) (That one doesn't count – *I* made that one up.) Finish conflicts today. Bonus: Do twenty multiple-choice questions on random subjects.

Day 47: PRACTICAL TEST and REVIEW. Do a ninety-minute practical test. Write out your full answer, and stop after ninety minutes. You might be done with studying for the practical test! If you are, review your hardest subjects, and do practice questions – multiple choice and essay, as appropriate – for them. If not, work on your practical test problem: issue spotting, rule writing, time management, whatever it is. Re-read the chapter below on the practical test for refreshment or insight.

Day 48: TORTS, CIV PRO, CRIM PRO, EVIDENCE, & CON LAW. Morning: Review the law of torts, civil procedure, criminal law and procedure, evidence, and constitutional law. Caution: Staring at the page might not be effective review. Afternoon: Outline essay answers in those subjects. Then do multiple-choice questions in those areas. If you do not have subject-matter specific multiple-choice questions, do multiple-choice questions in all subject areas. *Look up the correct answers for the questions you got wrong.*

Day 49. CONTRACTS, PROPERTY, BUS. ASSOCS., & SEC. TRANS. Morning: Review the law of contracts, real property, business associations, and secured transactions. (Do NOT keep staring at the page if that is putting you to sleep. Outline essay questions to keep your alertness instead, if necessary.) Afternoon: Outline essays in contracts, real property, business associations, and secured transactions. Do multiple-choice questions in contracts and real property, or in all subjects.

Day 50: FAMILY, TRUSTS & ESTATES, CONFLICTS, & HARD SUBJECTS. Morning: Review the law in family law, trusts and estates, conflicts, and in your hardest subjects. Afternoon: Outline essays in family law, trusts and estates, and conflicts. Outline essays in your hardest subjects. Get a good night's rest.

Day 51: TEST DAY. Morning: Do a three-and-a-half-hour essay test covering each of torts, civil procedure, criminal law and procedure, evidence, constitutional law, contracts, and real property, allotting thirty minutes to each subject. Make the exam conditions as realistic as possible. Look up the model answers for each question after the three-and-a-half hours. Enjoy your greater stamina and considerable knowledge. Feels good, doesn't it? Afternoon: Do a ninety-minute practical test (if you feel you need to) AND/OR outline answers to essay questions in your hardest subjects. Then look up the model answers. Go for speed in organizing what you will write. Can you analyze a question and outline an answer in ten minutes, leaving you twenty minutes to write your butt off?

Day 52: TEST DAY. Morning: Do a three-hour multiple-choice test on all subjects. Make the exam conditions as realistic as possible, filling in bubbles to answer questions, and stopping when time is up. How is your time management? Are you putting the answers next to the correct numbers? Are you seeing your score improve? Isn't it wonderful?!? Look up answers to the questions you got wrong, and study why the right answer is the right answer. Afternoon: Do fifty-question timed batches of multiple-choice questions, and study the correct answers. Review any vague areas of the law.

Day 53: Travel Day. Review everything. Relax. Marathoners taper off the days before the Big Run. For attorney candidates, tapering means light review of everything, especially the hard subjects.

Feel the knowledge coursing through your veins. Visualize success on the bar exam. Make sure you have all the paperwork, identification, clear plastic sandwich bag, pens, pencils, laptop and software, gasoline, snacks, water, medicine, etc., that you will need for entrance to and participation in the bar exam. Read and understand the directions for the essay test and for the practical test that you will take tomorrow. Know how and when you will get to the bar exam venue itself. Eat a good dinner and get a good night's sleep. *You got this!*

Day 54: EXAM DAY: Essays and Practical Test. Aim to get there early. Remember to breathe, to manage your time, and to write your answers in the right places. Afterwards, look up the law to a question or two, if you must. Then relax: your essays and practical test answers are in the bag! Lightly review the subjects for the multiple-choice test. Do no more than twenty random multiple-choice questions, just to get your mind pivoted to the new exam format. Feel all the relevant knowledge and techniques flooding back. Prepare your pencils, identification, clear plastic sandwich bag, etc., for the morning. Read the instructions for the multiple-choice test you will take tomorrow. Eat a good meal, and get a good night's rest.

Day 55: EXAM DAY: Multiple-Choice Test. Aim to get there early. Manage your time, and mark your answers next to the correct number. Check that often. Remember to breathe. Then you are done! With all of your hard work and a little Grace from Above, ***you will never have to take another bar exam!***

The foregoing calendar list is a suggestion. Notice how the bar exam happens on Days 54 and 55 – your timeline could be different by a day or three. (The foregoing calendar list aligns perfectly if Day 1 is June 1st, and June 1st is a Sunday.) The subjects are fewer than those I encountered on the South Carolina and Virginia bar exams. Build your own calendar. You will see from my proposed calendar list, however, a few useful techniques, I hope. Key among those techniques: *practice early and often!* Studying black letter law is rather boring if you have no purpose driving it beyond a vague "I-wanna-pass-the-bar-exam." An early view of the questions you will face will inform you and inspire you (initially scare the *poop* out of you) to seek effective internalization and utilization efforts.

B. Actual Studying: How Do You Get All This Stuff in Your Head?

In my calendar list, I say things like, "study for internalization" or "study constitutional law." What does that mean, to study effectively?

Knowledge is a little bit like dirt. The more you play with it, the more it sticks to you. You have got to play with the dirt that is the knowledge you need on the bar exam in ways that efficiently make it stick. Happily, you have had three or four years of law school learning how to make it stick. So go with what works. "Oh, but the bar exam is different!" you shriek. "Law school exams covered just one subject at a time. The bar exam covers everything! How am I going to get all the knowledge in the world about law in my head?!?" Let me encourage you, Dear Reader, that you have proven *beyond a shadow of a reasonable doubt* that you have what it takes to get the requisite knowledge in your head in a way that will allow you to call upon it, *to command it,* to do your will and earn you points on the bar exam. In fact, I submit to you that the unfortunate souls who do not pass the bar exam on the first attempt did not fail for lack of studying the law; rather, and this is the thesis of this book, *they failed to practice enough.* More on practice below.

How to study? Different techniques work for different people. I strongly suggest that you use several different techniques to create a multi-media approach. Read some, outline some, listen to a lecture some. Read concise outlines. Read detailed outlines. Write your own comprehensive outlines. Write your own "if all I knew about this area of the law was this little bit" outlines. (If all I knew about family law, it would be "do whatever is in the best interest of the child.") (Okay, there's more to family law, of course. But when you write your "if all I knew about this area of the law" outline, you may feel a sense of relief that you have learned something and can survive an essay question in that area of the law.) (Could you have written that outline a month ago?) Try flashcards. Whatever you do, DO NOT merely prepare beautiful, detailed outlines or other study materials in two dozen areas of the law, concluding that effort the day before the bar exam. The exam does not test you on how well you can write an outline of the law!

Please, please, please, Dear Reader, study AND practice! Study some, and practice some. I suggest that you will be more successful if you study some and practice some *each day*. You will find that your practice will make your study more efficient and more effective.

One plan you might follow is to attend or view some lectures such as those provided by Bar/Bri®, Kaplan, Inc., and others. Then that same day, attempt to practice outlining an essay question or answer some multiple-choice questions on the subject matter of the lecture.

But not everyone can afford those lecture courses. You must find source materials for the black-letter law that you must internalize, and practice questions galore. I am becoming a huge fan of the National Conference of Bar Examiners. They provide a wealth of information about their exams, from study aids, to online practice tests, to statistics on who is taking and passing the bar exam. I urge you to go to their website and poke around: NCBEX.org. They will write the bar exam you will probably take, so their materials are pretty much straight from the horse's mouth. I wish I had been aware of their resources back when I took my bar exams (insert geezer cough here). (I suspect those online materials were not available back then.)

Here's how I studied. For my first bar exam, I would attend a lecture (Bar/Bri®, huge fan) and take notes as best I could. (My handwriting is terrible.) Then within a half-hour of finishing the lecture, I would review my notes and fill in blanks in my notes, often with really good recollection of what I just heard in lecture. Or, for later bar exams where lectures were not an option for me, I would read outlines of black-letter law, either commercially-available outlines or detailed outlines prepared by friends who had taken the exam before. (If you are relying on outlines prepared by friends, get at least two of them. If one friend misses one detail, the other friend might catch it.) I made a point of reading through outlines for all of the subjects on the bar exam, even if I had attended a lecture on a given subject.

I also made an outline, but it was concise. I would take a sheet of legal paper (of course!) and write in small print those keywords that reflected the rule. I would write, for example, on my torts outline, "Negligence: Duty. Breach. Causation. Damages. Causation = Reasonably Foreseeable (minority: But For)." I would also annotate my outline with page numbers or other indications so I could look back at the original source in case my keyword outline was incomplete or confusing. Then, as the bar exam drew closer and closer, I would review my outlines, perhaps before practicing essays in those subjects. Importantly, I would also dive back into the detailed outlines in my source materials, sometimes for specific questions, and other times just for fun. (Ha. Ha.)

The key for me was that I was working with the knowledge, and thereby getting it to stick to me like dirt. Reading sometimes put me to sleep. Attending lectures helped me, but was complete by about mid-June. Avoid getting into a rut: There you are, doing something that is not really effective at getting the material in your brain, but you sure feel good that "Boy, oh boy, we sure are studying!" Try different things. And have I mentioned the need to practice?

C. Practice, Practice, Practice! (Run, Run, Run!)

Imagine that by Exam Day, all you have done is outlined the law. Or you have merely read outlines. That is the marathon equivalent of merely writing, or merely reading, a book about running. And then you have to go run a marathon! Your mind and, importantly, your body, are not ready for the task at hand. Another analogy: suppose you are taking a guitar class or a piano class, and your final exam, upon which your entire grade rests, consists of a recital. You do NOT want to show up at the recital having *only read about how to play your instrument.* No. You want to practice so much that your recital goes *flawlessly*, that it is almost anti-climactic because you have prepared, *practiced*, so thoroughly.

My Dear Reader, for successful marathons, musical recitals, and bar exams, your mind and body need callouses in all the right places. How do you get those callouses? That's right: PRACTICE.

I recall my first practice essay. I gave myself forty-five minutes to write my magnum opus, just like I would have on Exam Day (essays were longer on that bar exam). I diligently located the question at the end of the fact pattern, read the fact pattern, and outlined my answer. My essay was going to be great. But thirty minutes had passed! I began writing furiously! I had finished only half of my essay when time expired. I still recall the feeling of shock and horror I felt from that first practice essay. Happily, that happened in June, and I had plenty of time to recover. If your first essay goes the same way, do not worry. Just don't let your first essay be on Exam Day.

Early in your preparation schedule, practice answering essay questions fully. On those early essays, be cognizant of the time, but do not worry about meeting the time limit. Build speed later. Also, if on an early practice essay question, you have absolutely no clue how to even begin your answer, go ahead and peek. Peek at your source materials, outline, flashcards, what have you, to find any relevant rule of law. Peek at the model answer. If it is not inside your head, go outside your head to find the answer. "Oh!" you should say. "THAT's what this question seeks as an answer!" Study the rules of law that govern, now that you have seen the fact pattern. Study the model answer. Begin to match in your mind the fact pattern to the model answer. You should start to see, or even just feel, that when the question looks like this, the model answer looks like that.

Immediately after looking up the rules of law or model answer, outline and write your essay as if the rule of law came from inside your head. Later in your preparation, work hard to peek less and less. Write out your full answer before looking up the rules of law or the model answer. Practice this way and you will get better and better at answering questions in the time allotted.

The same goes for practical tests. On your first attempt, you may have to peek at the model answer. Immediately upon seeing the model answer, close the book and write your own answer. "Oh!" you will say. "That's what it feels like to write a correct answer." You will get better and better as time goes on. Go for speed later on, working to stay within the time allowed.

For multiple-choice questions, start off with small batches of questions focused in a single subject if you can. Do ten, for example, and don't worry about how long it takes. When you are finished those ten questions, immediately look up the correct answers for the questions you missed and work hard to determine why the correct answers are the correct answers. Also look up the answers for the questions you got right, to make sure your lucky guesses turn into honest wins supported by legal knowledge. Later, work for time. On the multiple-choice exam itself, you have one minute and forty-eight seconds, or 1.8 minutes, for each question. So do ten questions in eighteen minutes. Or twenty questions in thirty-six minutes. And then immediately work to learn the correct answers to the questions you got wrong.

By mid-February or mid-July, you should attempt multiple questions in a row, and even up to three-hour practice exams. Try two, and then four, and then six essay questions in a row. Try two ninety-minute practical tests in a row. Try one hour, then two hours, then three hours of multiple-choice tests. If your brain turns to mush after two hours of testing, find that out before Exam Day! Build that stamina! Learn what it takes to survive three hours of testing. Sure, you may be allowed to use a restroom during the three hours of an exam session. AVOID NEEDING TO DO THAT! Importantly, plan your nutrition and hydration for Exam Day so you are not fainting from hunger or thinking about dehydration instead of the finer points of apparent versus inherent agency authority.

By practicing, you accomplish several things. You train your mind to correctly process the question. You train your body to answer the question. Writing an exam for six hours a day exhausts the untrained mind and body. You build your mind and body into an efficient machine that can answer each question in the time allotted, and to complete the entire exam in the time allotted without petering out at the end.

D. Over and Over

Practice as much as you can. That means several practice essays in each subject. Some you will write out in full, to practice those essay-writing skills. But also practice only outlining, to get exposure to as many fact patterns as possible. Practice your multiple-choice questions by the thousands. Yes, thousands. You will thank me later.

It is my sense that the practical test does not need as much practice. Once you get the concept of how to answer a practical test, and you have done a few timed practice practical tests, you should be good. Spend your time instead internalizing substantive law and practicing your essays and your multiple-choice questions.

The skills you develop practicing are as important as the law you internalize by studying. The bar exam challenges you mentally and physically, and you can master it only by training your mind and body with practice.

There are several sources for practice exam materials. The creators of the Uniform Bar Examination and the components thereof offer a wealth of practice materials online (NCBEX.org), including actual past exams and model answers. And there exist several additional high-quality sources of practice materials. (Internet search: bar exam practice tests.) Seek practice questions that are separated by subject, as well as practice questions with subject matters mixed together, as they will be on Exam Day. Make sure that model answers accompany essay questions and practical tests, and correct answers, preferably with explanations, accompany multiple-choice questions. The bar exam will seem anti-climactic, because you will have seen it all before.

III. Essays

A. Introduction to Essays

The essay portion of the bar exam typically consists of six essay questions, each allotted thirty minutes, over the course of three hours. A question usually focuses on a single area of the law, but concepts and even rules of law from other areas of the law may be implicated in the question. A fact pattern presents a hypothetical situation, and then a question (or three) directs the attorney candidate to make some determination as to the legal rights or outcome of a law suit based on the fact pattern. The collection of essay questions explores a variety of subjects in the law, from family law to business associations.

If a bar exam tested only whether you had legal knowledge, the exam might contain exclusively multiple-choice questions, perhaps. But a real live lawyer needs to analyze legal issues and reach legal conclusions using that legal knowledge. Also, the lawyer needs to communicate that analysis and those conclusions, often with the goal of persuading the reader. True, the correct answers in a multiple-choice test require at least some legal analysis. But the correct answer to any particular multiple-choice question completely hides whether it was obtained through sound legal analysis or by pure dumb luck. An answer to an essay question, on the other hand, simultaneously reveals the attorney candidate's legal knowledge, legal analysis ability, and written communication ability.

Essay answers that have not earned sufficient points to pass the bar exam suffer, in my view, from two shortcomings. The first, largest shortcoming is that the answer does not have sufficient structure. The attorney candidate has failed to build enough skeleton upon which to hang the muscle and organs of the answer. What tidbits of legal knowledge and legal analysis the candidate has placed on the page settle into a squishy pile that no bar examiner can credit. The second shortcoming, minor in comparison, is an apparent lack of legal knowledge. There is barely enough meat on the bones to show the attorney candidate knows anything. I suspect that it is merely the lack of structure that stops candidates from passing, and the apparent lack of legal knowledge in the answer stems merely from the lack of anywhere logical to put the considerable legal knowledge the candidate truly has.

Let me teach you how to structure your essay answers. This is where your ability to reason like a lawyer will shine. And your vast legal knowledge will find a suitable place to emerge to the bar examiners' point-giving delight.

B. Structure Your Essay: Answer, Issue, Rule, Analysis, Conclusion: "AIRAC"

Just as human beings all have the same basic skeletal structure, every single legal issue that you address on the bar exam should have the same basic structure. You will address major issues, and you will address minor issues. Each and every issue should be addressed with the same structure. Importantly, the structure reveals your ability to think like a lawyer, or more specifically, to analyze a legal issue. The structure I propose states the answer, the issue, the rule of law, your analysis, and your conclusion. The acronym AIRAC summarizes the structure nicely.

Consider the following template:

A. The answer is X.
I. The issue is whether Y is true or false.
R. In this jurisdiction, Y is true when elements A, B, and C are present.
A. In this case, A is present. B is present. C is present. Accordingly, Y is true.
C. In conclusion, X is the answer since Y is true because A, B, and C are present.

Every essay answer that you write should conform or contain that rather formulaic structure. This is helpful on the bar exam to the extent that you do not have to invent a structure for your answer in addition to having to invent the answer itself.

Here is another way to express the AIRAC template:

A. [The answer is _______.]
I. The issue here is _____________.
R. In [your state], [the rule is __________].
A. In this case, [analyze whether the facts meet *each element* of the rule, and use all of the evidence].
C. In conclusion, [re-answer the question] ________________, because [give a reason] _____________.

Let me elaborate.

Answer. Bar examiners, clients, and judges all want one thing in particular: an answer. Accordingly, *answer the question.* Who wins the lawsuit? Can the defendant prove an adequate alibi? Does the plaintiff state a claim upon which relief can be granted? The first sentence of your answer should completely answer the question being asked. Do not write "yes" or "no," but rather restate the main question as a sentence giving a definite answer. "The plaintiff wins the lawsuit because a preponderance of the evidence shows the defendant's negligence." "The defendant cannot prove an adequate alibi because she has only circumstantial evidence suggesting she was at the movies, while direct evidence shows she was at the scene of the crime." "The plaintiff adequately states a claim for medical malpractice, since all elements of that claim are met in the present circumstances." The clue to starting your answer sentence appears most likely in the final sentence of the essay question. Look for the sentence that ends with a question mark. If none exists, look for an imperative sentence such as, "Explain why the court should not dismiss this case at the present stage of the litigation." Your answer sentence in this example might start with: "The court should not dismiss this case at the present stage of the litigation because ________." Simple, right? You have already earned a few points, just by answering the question!

Issue. State the issue to show the bar examiners that you are indeed a law school graduate. Do so in a sentence that informs that you are stating the issue. "The issue is

______." Even underline the word, "issue." Often, there are several issues raised in a fact pattern for an essay question. It is often simplest to deal with the issues one at a time. Apply AIRAC to the first, most-important issue, and then apply AIRAC to the next issue, and so on, until you have addressed all of the major issues. As time allows, apply AIRAC to the minor issues, too.

Rule. State the rule or rules of law that apply to your issue. Signal to the bar examiners that you are stating the rule by starting the sentence with, "In this jurisdiction," "In West Dakota [*i.e.,* the state in which you are applying for bar membership]," or the like. You might write just the two-letter abbreviation for your state to save you time: "In WD, [the rule of law is ______]."

What do you do if you forget the rule, or do not know the rule? *Make up a rule.* You know enough about the law, and will have internalized enough law to at least guess at the proper structure of a rule that governs any fact pattern that any bar exam question might throw at you. I have *never* regurgitated with statutory perfection the entire rule on any essay question in any jurisdiction for which I have passed the bar. In your law practice, you will research the statutes, regulations, and case law to quote with precision the latest and greatest articulation of the rules of law that govern your clients' matters. On the bar exam, however, nobody expects that kind of precision. If you jumble the wording a little bit, or even miss an element, you will not suffer too badly for it. Of course, do not forget the element upon which the question turns!

"Oh, no," you say. "I cannot make up a rule!" Where do you think rules came from in the first place? Someone, once upon a time, saw a fact pattern and sat down and *made up a rule* to govern what should happen in that circumstance. That is the whole premise of our common law legal system: we trust judges to sit around and make up rules. "It is emphatically the province and duty of the judicial department to say what the law is." *Marbury v. Madison,* 5 U.S. (1 Cranch) 137 (1803).

How do you get good at making up rules? *Practice.* Run, run, run!

Analysis. Apply the law to the facts of the question. Signal to the bar examiners that you are starting the analysis with, "In this case," or "Here," for example. Then address each and every element that you put into your rule. It is that simple.

How do you know what is an element of a rule? Look at each word and see whether it (or groups of words) creates its own item the prosecutor or plaintiff has to prove. Alternatively, look at each word or group of words and ask, "Could a defendant escape the claim by saying that word or group of words in the rule was absent in fact?"

Consider the rule: "A defendant is guilty of speeding if the defendant was driving a motor vehicle in excess of a posted speed limit." Let us find the elements of that rule. Was the defendant driving? Was it a motor vehicle? Was the speed of the vehicle excessive? What was the speed limit? Was it posted? Each of those questions identifies a separate element that must be addressed in your essay. As you practice your essay writing, and indeed on the bar exam itself, it may be helpful to number the elements as you write the rule. "A defendant is guilty of speeding if the (1) defendant (2) was driving (3) a motor vehicle (4) in excess of (5) a posted (6) speed limit." Number the elements at least when you outline your essay (*see* "Attacking an Essay Question" below).

Do not forget about auxiliary matters such as burdens of proof and standards of review on appeal, as appropriate. If necessary or useful, incorporate them into your articulation of the rule. "A defendant is guilty of speeding if *the State can prove beyond a shadow of a reasonable doubt that* the defendant was driving a motor vehicle in excess of a posted speed limit." Alternatively, work the burden of proof into your analysis. "It appears the State can show *beyond a shadow of a reasonable doubt* that the defendant met the excessive speed element given the radar gun's reading of 95 m.p.h., and the recent calibration of the radar gun." Or, more clearly: "The defendant met the excessive speed element given the radar gun's reading of 95 m.p.h. The recent calibration of the radar gun, and defendant's lack of opposing evidence, proves excessive speed *beyond a shadow of a reasonable doubt*."

Occasionally, you can garner additional points by dealing with a rule followed by other jurisdictions, such as the minority rule. If you have time, it could be useful to apply AIRAC to discuss that other rule. Do it quickly, because that rule does not control in your jurisdiction.

Conclusion. State your conclusion, and give a reason. "In conclusion, the court should not issue an injunction in this case, because money damages will adequately compensate the plaintiff." The conclusion will sound similar to the answer, and could be the same. If your answer fully addresses the question, as it should, the conclusion might even be omitted. Include a conclusion only if it adds new information (*i.e.,* gathers more points!). Re-read your answer sentence at the beginning of your essay. If your answer sentence is a bit thin, but fully answers the question, add a conclusion that includes a reason. For example, if the question is, "Who wins?" an adequate answer is, "The plaintiff wins the lawsuit." The conclusion should read, in this example, something like, "The plaintiff wins the lawsuit because a preponderance of the evidence shows the defendant's negligence."

Put it all together. Internalize the AIRAC structure and use it every chance you get in the days between now and the bar exam. "What time is it?" asks your beloved, seemingly ignorant of the mere fifty-something days between now and the bar exam, and the palpable sense of impending doom hanging in the air. Impress your beloved with your ability to structure your answer like a real live lawyer: "[Answer] The time is three o'clock. [Issue] The issue is, what is the current time? [Rule] In this jurisdiction, time is determined by the position of the hands of an accurately-set clock or watch. [Analysis] In this case, the clock on the wall shows that the big hand is on the twelve, and the little hand is on the three. The time on that clock matches the time on my smart phone, which is corrected whenever it receives a cellular signal. Accordingly, the clock on the wall is accurately set. [Conclusion] In conclusion, the present time as given by the accurately-set clock on the wall is three o'clock."

C. Issue Spotting

Okay, okay. Essay questions are not always as easy as telling the time. Answering them successfully will require you to work diligently and efficiently for the entire time allotted. Often, an essay question will ask you to balance competing interests. For example, in a fact pattern involving a contract, one party might breach, and then the other party breaches in retaliation. Who wins the lawsuit between them? Only sound legal analysis will tell. How do you decide what to analyze? Issue spotting!

A key to balancing the competing interests is the ability to identify separate issues. In the mutual-breach-of-contract example above, one or several issues will swirl around the first party's breach. Was it a breach? Was it justified? What are the acceptable remedies available to the non-breaching party? Let us suppose that the first party's breach was actually a breach, and unjustified, and the non-breaching party's remedies did not include breaching in retaliation.

Now we look to the second party's breach. Was it actually a breach? Was it justified, by the first party's breach or otherwise? What remedies are available to the first party because of the second party's breach? Does the first party lose any of those remedies because the first party breached? Look at all the issues that leap to mind, and we don't know anything about the case except that two parties breached a contract! Those issues leap to mind because we know a little bit about contract law. (If anything looked surprising or foreign in this paragraph, don't worry! By Exam Day, your mind will be brimming with legal knowledge and issues will leap off the page at you!)

Indeed, issues will leap off the page when you read the fact pattern. Any one issue could fill a chapter in a casebook. How do you manage all of those issues? You have to develop a sense of which issues are the most important – which issues are **dispositive**. Once you have dealt with the dispositive issue or issues, deal with as many further issues as you can to obtain as many points as you can. Then, when time runs out for that question, turn to the next question.

How can you tell which issues are important, dispositive, or should be dealt with first? Let me give you a fact pattern to practice your issue-spotting skills:

> One day, Shopkeeper, the owner of a consumer electronics store, was tending his store and noticed a shopper, Suspect, lingering at the display of a portable game console that retails for $1,000. Shopkeeper noticed Suspect standing there for approximately five minutes. When the suspect walked away, Shopkeeper walked over to the

display and noticed an empty box for the portable game console opened and on the floor near the display. Shopkeeper hurried after Suspect and saw suspect pulling his hand from his jacket pocket as Suspect passed the cash registers on the way out the door.

Shopkeeper yelled, "Stop!" and seized Suspect by the elbow. "What's in your pocket?" demanded Shopkeeper. "Nothing," answered Suspect, but refused to allow Shopkeeper to search Suspect's pockets. Shopkeeper led Suspect by the elbow to an office next to the cash registers, entered the office with Suspect, closed the door, and phoned police to request an officer. Shopkeeper stood at the door to the office with his arms crossed, blocking Suspect from leaving, for twenty minutes before Police Officer arrived to question Suspect. Police Officer frisked and searched Suspect, and found no stolen merchandise in Suspect's pockets. Police Officer let

> Suspect go. Suspect sued Shopkeeper for false imprisonment. Will Suspect win on his claim for false imprisonment?

What issue or issues are dispositive? In our suspected shoplifting case, it is more important that there was no evidence on Suspect's person that he attempted to steal anything. It is less important the value of the goods the shopkeeper suspected were lifted. Accordingly, the most important, dispositive issues in the shoplifting case involve the shopkeeper's actions vis à vis the suspect's innocence. Did the shopkeeper act reasonably? Did the shopkeeper injure the suspect? "The issue is whether the shopkeeper acted reasonably in detaining the person he suspected of shoplifting." Do you see that issue? Hopefully, also you can see how that issue might lead you to state a rule. "In this jurisdiction, a shopkeeper can detain a suspect for a reasonable amount of time and under reasonable circumstances if the shopkeeper has a genuine belief that the suspect has attempted to steal merchandise from the shopkeeper's store." Indeed, stating the dispositive issue should lead you to a full AIRAC outline and an essay.

Now, if you deal with that issue soundly, but you still have five minutes left, you might raise the minor issue of the value of the goods. The more valuable the goods, the more significant the crime, right? You can use this minor issue to augment your analysis of the major issue: what is a reasonable detention for a stolen electronic device worth $1,000 might not be reasonable for a stolen pack of gum. And your jurisdiction probably has a penal distinction between them – a felony for one, and a misdemeanor for the other. Use the five minutes you have left to show off your knowledge, and gain a few more points.

What does treatment of a minor issue look like in practice? It should look like AIRAC.

Some more tips on issue spotting: consider the evidentiary burdens, the posture of the case, and the standards of review on appeal. Those are likely never the major issue in an essay question, but many points can be had if you spot them and address them. Use AIRAC to address each of them that time allows.

D. All Elements Rule

Perhaps the single best tip I can give you, Dear Reader, appears in what I call the "All Elements Rule." In my personal, law school, and professional life, I have had very dramatic experiences that have lead me to articulate this rule for you.

My first exposure to the rule involved a rescue I performed as a lifeguard. A child slipped under the water in front of my lifeguard chair on the first day of summer, and I pulled him out and my fellow lifeguards and I gave him CPR and then rescue breathing once we detected a pulse. We cracked a rib, but he was breathing on his own by the time the ambulance collected him. The child was fine, ultimately, and Thank God For That!

A trial ensued. After the plaintiff rested, the judge gave me my first lesson in the All Elements Rule. Negligence requires (1) duty, (2) breach, (3) causation, and (4) damages. Here, the regulations held that a lifeguard has a duty to scan his area once a minute. I testified that I had scanned the area once every thirty seconds. (I didn't know the rule beforehand, promise!) So there was no breach of the duty to scan. But even if there was, there had to be damages resulting from the breach. The child's injuries, assuming that he had in fact lost his heartbeat (questionable because chest compressions alone are unlikely to restart a stopped heart), and along with a cracked rib, were all consistent with a lifeguard performing his duty and scanning the area at least once a minute. The Bad, Bad Thing that happened to that child could have happened within the space of a minute, so at least two elements, breach and damages, had not been shown. Case dismissed.

Okay, now back to bar exam preparation. The All Elements Rule means that you have to address all of the elements in your rule. Do this every single time, for every single rule, in every single opportunity on the bar exam. I will mention the All Elements Rule again when we talk about the practical test – it is that important. This single skill, or rather exercise in self-discipline, determines who passes the bar exam and who does not.

When you recite a rule, number of the elements in your outline. Write the rule in your AIRAC outline, and then go back and put a little number above each element. Then, when you are writing your analysis in your answer, cross off those elements that you have addressed. It is that simple.

Consider what it looks like in real life, if you do not follow the All Elements Rule. There you are, going on and on about how three of the four elements of negligence are met, for example. You rest your case, and your opposing counsel stands up and moves to dismiss. The judge immediately grants the motion to dismiss, because you have presented no evidence whatsoever that a crucial element has been met in the current circumstances.

This almost happened to me in law school. I was trying a case in my trial advocacy course that involved an allegation of armed robbery. I had gotten all kinds of testimony and evidence admitted relating to all of the elements except for the value of goods stolen. The rule was something like, "A person commits the felony of armed robbery if he forces a victim to surrender an article of value while the person displays or brandishes a lethal weapon." On the motion to dismiss after I rested the prosecution's case, the judge lectured me on the missing element of value. Sure, the victim testified that she surrendered her purse. Purses have value, don't they? No, they don't, unless you prove they do!

The judge denied the motion to dismiss, however, because my police officer witness testified as to the money that was in the purse, and the defense did not object to that hearsay testimony. (I suspect the judge also denied the motion so that the defense would have the pleasure of presenting their case and earning their grade.) Let us look at the rule again, and identify the elements: "A person commits the felony of armed robbery if (1) he forces (2) a victim (3) to surrender (4) an article (5) of value (6) while the person (7) displays or brandishes (8) a lethal weapon." Numbering the elements during your outlining will allow you to remember to address each element in your answer.

I won't tell you the times in my professional life when the All Elements Rule reared its ugly/beautiful head. But trust me – the bar examiners do not want a person cavorting about in civilized society, pretending to be a lawyer, if that person cannot follow the All Elements Rule.

E. All Evidence Suggestion

Use all the evidence in your fact pattern. I call this the All Evidence Suggestion. Just as the All Elements Rule gives you the discipline to fully analyze the entire rule of law governing your fact pattern, the All Evidence Suggestion gives you the discipline to fully analyze all the evidence in your fact pattern. Moreover, this will show a certain maturity in your analysis: you can deal with "bad facts," or with facts that do not support or even refute your conclusion. I call this the All Evidence Suggestion because it should not be adhered to as strictly as the All Elements Rule. Violate the All Elements Rule and you do not pass the bar exam. Omit reference to minor details in the fact pattern in harmless violation of the All Evidence Suggestion, and you still ace the bar exam.

One way to follow the All Evidence Suggestion is to number or circle the bits of evidence in your fact pattern. Then cross them off when you have used them in your essay. Of course, do not obliterate them, because you might need to see them again when you deal with another issue.

Be sure to raise and deal with facts and arguments that go against your conclusion. Consider the Shopkeeper and the Suspect in the electronics store. If you ignore the fact that no device was found in Suspect's pocket, Suspect looks guilty, guilty, guilty. But no court could convict Suspect because of that one little factoid: Suspect didn't have the game console on his person. By considering every bit of evidence, you avoid a wrong conclusion, such as: "Suspect will not prevail on his claim of false imprisonment, because Suspect is guilty of attempted larceny." Oops. That sentence would send up a Little Red Flag for the bar examiners. Accordingly, the All Elements Suggestion will allow everything in the fact pattern to make its way into your answer, in a coherent, organized, you-deserve-to-be-a-lawyer-darn-it kind of way.

F. Unknown Subject Matter

On the Virginia bar exam, I encountered a question addressing an area of the law that I had not studied at all. The fact pattern, in my estimation, called for the defense of entrapment. *Entrapment*.

Holy smokes! In all of my preparation, for every one of my bar exams, and in four years of evening law school, I had *never* encountered the entrapment defense. My dim awareness of that defense probably came from a childhood spent watching cops and robbers on TV. Didn't they know that I was a *registered patent lawyer?* That I won't need criminal law until my kids are *teenagers?* So what did I do? More germane, what will you do, Dear Reader, when you encounter something that you have never seen before?

You already know what to do. First, outline your answer using AIRAC. Answer the question: "The defendant is not guilty [of the charged offense] because he can prove an entrapment defense." (I apologize, Dear Reader, that copyright law stops me from elucidating the fact pattern here.) Now state the issue: "The issue here is whether the defendant has adequate evidence to prove his entrapment defense." Now *make up some rules*: "In this state, [the charged offense consists of elements A, B, C.] However, a defense of entrapment can defeat a criminal charge if the defendant can prove [by clear and convincing evidence?] that he was coerced by an authority to perform the acts constituting the charged offense. [I still have no idea if that rule is correct]." Once you have constructed a rule, finish your outline.

Analysis in your outline will be sparse, and the conclusion reiterates and adds to the answer.

Now it is time to write your essay. Follow your outline. Once you are happy with the rule that you have constructed, put it out of your mind that you have made it up. To enhance your essay and earn more points, consider elucidating the burden of proof that falls on the prosecution for proving the count, and the burden of proof that falls on the defendant for proving his defense. Line up every piece of evidence, both for and against the count, and for and against the defense.

You can use your imagination to introduce more evidence if you get desperate. For example, the defendant may bring in character witnesses to attest to his good character. And note in your answer that introducing character witnesses may open the door for the prosecution to introduce evidence of prior convictions. For another example, perhaps the defendant's wife or best friend can testify to conversations with the defendant before the sting about the circumstances leading to the defendant's arrest. (Hearsay?) A word of caution, however: be very careful to use every piece of evidence in the fact pattern before you go about suggesting additional evidence.

In my answer, I recall writing a few sentences about how every criminal conviction requires proof of an actus reus ("evil act") and a mens rea ("evil mind"). Here, because the defendant was coerced into committing the acts constituting the crime, the defendant did not have the requisite mens rea to be convicted for possession with intent to distribute. The point is that your answer must show the bar examiners that you have sufficient knowledge, analytical skill, and communication ability to serve society as a lawyer, not that you know how to memorize.

G. Attacking an Essay Question

When you are allowed to look at your essay question, first determine the question you have to answer. Typically, that is the last sentence of the fact pattern. Often, you will not be surprised to learn that it ends with a question mark. Sometimes, however, there will be more than one question that you have to answer. Usually, if there is a multi-part question, each part will have its own letter. For example, "(a) Who wins the lawsuit, if the court believes the first witness? (b) Who wins the lawsuit, if the court believes the second witness? (c) Who wins the lawsuit, if the video evidence clearly shows that the defendant was actually trying to help the plaintiff before the gun went off?" Skim through the fact pattern to ensure that there are not additional questions buried somewhere in the middle of the fact pattern.

Now that you know the question or number of questions that you have to answer, decide how much time you have. For a three-part question on a thirty-minute essay, you have approximately ten minutes per question, right? That is one way to look at it, and I will tell you that allotting ten minutes per question at least gives you a chance to fully address the questions. Consider how you would feel if you spent thirty minutes answering the first part, only to discover to your horror that there were two more parts to answer. I did this once during law school, and wrote a beautiful answer that was worth only ten points. I am sure that I got all ten points on that part, but my failure to plan ahead caused me to write very short answers for the remaining parts of a forty-point question.

But let us refine our time allotment here. You might give yourself, for example, fifteen minutes for the first part and just seven and a half minutes for each of the remaining two parts, to acknowledge that you don't have to read the fact pattern three times with the same care to answer each part. If necessary, write in your test booklet the time at which you must complete your answer to one part and move on to the next part – say, for an essay that starts at 10 AM, you write "10:15," "10:22:30," and "10:30." Concluding your efforts on one part and moving onto the next part reflects a beautiful truth of the bar exam: once your time has expired, you might never have to deal with that area of the law ever again, unless you really want to!

Now it is time to tackle outlining the first question. By all means, write out your new favorite acronym: AIRAC. But write it down the page in the white space in your test booklet, like this:

A
I
R
A
C

Next to the first A, write the answer to your question. Use shorthand if you can, and write only enough to spur you to write a full answer sentence in the answer booklet. Next to the I, write a word or words that identify the issue. Next to the R, write the rule out in full, and number the elements. This may be the only full sentence in your outline. Next to the second A, you might not need to write anything in your outline. Perhaps you will jot down an item of evidence to remind yourself to use it in your essay. Often, my outline was empty at this letter A, because my analysis during the actual essay writing was driven by the rule that I had written in full in my outline. Next to the C, write down a word or words to remind you of your conclusion.

If you spot another issue that needs to be addressed in your essay, write down another AIRAC outline. And repeat the foregoing exercise. Remember to always write out the entire rule in your outline, and number its elements. It is worth it! That way, your analysis will write itself when the time comes. If you shorthand the rule, you run the risk of forgetting an element when you are actually writing your essay.

Let me give you an example of an outline:

A – App'ant wins
I – Wr substantial evidence
R – (1) A jury verdict on (2) a question of fact cannot be reversed (3) on appeal if there is (4) subs. evid. to support jury verdict. Substantial evid. = (1) sufficient for (2) reasonable mind to (3) accept conclusion.
A – no matter if counter evid.

C – App'ant wins b/c no evidence supported jury verdict – only lawyer argument at closing.

From the foregoing outline, you can now see how the essay is going to be written – *how the essay is going to write itself!* Preparing the outline causes you to do a lot of the critical thinking that will help you write the answer. This saves you from having to do the critical thinking while you are also performing the mechanical task of writing your answer. The exception to this, of course, is in the analysis portion of the answer. But outlining in the foregoing way will allow you to conserve precious time by avoiding writing the analysis twice. There should be enough substance in your outline so that writing the analysis comes relatively easily.

Let us look at each line of the outline, so I can explain the thinking behind what is written.

A – App'ant wins: This obviously answers the question, which must look something like this: "Who wins the appeal [based on the foregoing fact pattern]?" Note that I referred to the party with the correct label. Since the posture of the case involves an appeal, the parties are no longer "plaintiff" and "defendant," but rather "appellant" and "respondent."

I – Wr substantial evidence: This shorthand should lead you to write, "The issue is whether substantial evidence supports the jury's verdict."

R – (1) A jury verdict on (2) a question of fact cannot be reversed (3) on appeal if there is (4) subs. evid. to support jury verdict. Substantial evid. = (1) sufficient for (2) reasonable mind to (3) accept conclusion: Well, those are the governing rules. It bears repeating: write out the rules in full and number the elements. Okay, I abbreviated a few words to save time. Make sure every word of each rule is represented in your outline, abbreviated or otherwise, so you do not omit any words from your rule written in your essay. The written rule in your outline becomes a mini-outline for your analysis.

A – no matter if counter evid.: There is not much need here to write out your analysis. You will stare at the rule in your outline when you write your analysis. The few words I have written will remind me of a point that I want to make that does not flow directly from the elements of the rule. After showing that each element of the rule is met in the facts set forth in the fact pattern, I will state, "It does not matter in this case that there is countervailing evidence, unless that countervailing evidence arises to the level of disrupting the substantial evidence supporting the verdict. Here, the lawyer's argument at closing provides no evidence to disrupt the substantial evidence supporting the verdict."

C – App'ant wins b/c no evidence supported jury verdict – only lawyer argument at closing: This is the conclusion, somewhat restating the answer but incorporating an additional reason that reveals that I can tell the difference between evidence and lawyer argument.

Now that your outline is done, glance at your watch. With practice, somewhere between five and seven-and-a-half minutes have gone by, out of the fifteen minutes you have allotted to this part of the question. That gives you at least seven-and-a-half minutes to write out your answer. Write for the full allotment of time you have set aside. Answer the question, AIRAC your essay, apply the law to the facts using the All Elements Rule, use as much evidence you can in accordance with the All Evidence Suggestion, and state your conclusion. Raise and handle any minor issues, and when the fifteen minutes expires, move on to the next question.

Look back at the fact pattern involving the Shopkeeper who detained the Suspect. Was it a reasonable detention, or false imprisonment? Here's what an essay might look like:

> "[Answer] Suspect will not win on his claim against Shopkeeper for false imprisonment. [Issue] The issue is whether the shopkeeper acted reasonably in detaining the person he suspected of shoplifting. [Rule] In this jurisdiction, a shopkeeper can detain a

suspect for a reasonable amount of time and under reasonable circumstances if the shopkeeper has a genuine belief that the suspect has attempted to steal merchandise from the shopkeeper's store. [Analysis] Here, Shopkeeper detained Suspect for twenty minutes, long enough for Police Officer to arrive. Shopkeeper promptly called for a police officer once he had detained Suspect in the office, so the amount of time of detention was reasonable. Shopkeeper led Suspect by the elbow to an office, which apparently did not injure Suspect. Shopkeeper detained Suspect in the office, where the Shopkeeper stood with his arms crossed blocking the door so Suspect could not leave the office. No other physical means were used to restrain Suspect. Because of the lack of injury or significant physical discomfort to Suspect, the circumstances of the detention were reasonable. The Shopkeeper held a genuine belief that Suspect attempted to steal a portable game console worth $1,000, because

Shopkeeper observed Suspect standing in front of the display of the consoles for five minutes, and then Shopkeeper noticed an empty box for such a console on the floor near the display. Shopkeeper also saw Suspect pull Suspect's hand from his pocket as Suspect walked passed the cash registers out the door. All of those facts caused the Shopkeeper to genuinely believe that Suspect had placed merchandise from Shopkeeper's store in Suspect's pocket in an attempt to steal that merchandise. [Conclusion] Suspect will not prevail on his claim of false imprisonment, because Shopkeeper held a genuine belief that Suspect had attempted to steal the portable game console, and because the Shopkeeper detained Suspect for a reasonable time under reasonable circumstances.

[Now I deal with the minor issue of the value of the goods suspected of being stolen:]

"[Answer] The value of the goods suspected of being stolen has no impact in this case. [Issue] Another issue here is whether the shopkeeper acted reasonably in light of the significant value of the portable game console the shopkeeper believed the suspect had stolen. [Rule] In this jurisdiction, it is a felony to steal, or to attempt to steal, goods worth $250 or more from a retail establishment. [Analysis] In this case, the shopkeeper believed that the suspect had placed a portable game console in his coat pocket. The shopkeeper found an empty box for the console on the floor in his retail establishment near where the shopkeeper had observed the suspect standing. The console was offered for retail sale at the Shopkeeper's shop for $1,000. The suspect had put his hand into his coat pocket, reasonably raising the suspicion of the shopkeeper that the suspect had, in fact, attempted to steal the console worth more than $250 from the shopkeeper's shop. Thus, the shopkeeper genuinely suspected the suspect was committing a felony. However, in fact, the suspect did not place the device in his pocket; at least, the device was not found in his pocket when the police officer searched him. While a more aggressive or intense detention could be viewed as reasonable by a jury given the device's considerable value and the suspicion of the shopkeeper that he had witnessed a felony, it is already shown above that the shopkeeper acted reasonably in detaining the suspect long enough for a police officer to arrive to search the suspect. [Conclusion] Because the considerable value of the console only makes the shopkeeper's action more reasonable, the suspect cannot win on his claim of false imprisonment in this case."

(Don't write "Answer," "Issue," "Rule," "Analysis," or "Conclusion" in your essay. I point them out here so you can see what AIRAC looks like.)

H. Attacking the Essays on the Bar Exam Itself

We all learned in second grade to "Follow Directions." Make sure you do that. At the beginning of each time period allotted to the essays, the exam proctors for the Virginia bar exam had us attorney candidates hold up the colored booklets in which we were to write our answers. I recall there was a gold booklet, a salmon booklet, a blue booklet, and a green booklet. "Everybody holding up the gold booklet?" asked the head proctor. "Now shake it." A thousand attorney candidates wondered the purpose of this exercise, their gold booklets flapping in the air. The proctor explained: "On the previous question, someone wrote their answer in the wrong booklet. **Please make sure you write your answer in the correct booklet."**

If you are color blind, fear not. The booklets were labeled with other identifying features. And if you still cannot tell, or are not certain, raise your hand and ask a proctor for assistance.

On the bar exam itself, time is your enemy and your friend. When time runs out, you are done. Make time work for you! Know the structure of your essay exam before you go into it. You do NOT want to spend precious time during the exam reading instructions – read those instructions beforehand if you can. (Exam proctors sometimes had us read the instructions before the exam started!) Get past exams and thoroughly digest the structure of the exam at your leisure. Then, quickly review the instructions when you are told to begin the exam to ensure that you are following those instructions!

I. Concise Instructions for Essay Questions

Concise instructions that synthesize all of the foregoing:

Know the structure of the exam before Exam Day.

Write your answer in the correct booklet/place.

Manage your time – know how much time you have for each essay question and each part of each essay question.

Find the question or questions you have to answer.

Read the fact pattern carefully.

Spot the issues.

Outline using AIRAC – write the rule in full and number the elements.

Write your essay. When you write the analysis, follow the All Elements Rule by ticking off the elements of the rule in your outline.

As you write the analysis, also remember the All Evidence Suggestion – use every piece of evidence from the fact pattern in your analysis.

Raise and deal with minor issues using AIRAC until your time runs out.

Then move on to the next question.

IV. Practical Test

A. Introduction to the Practical Test

The practical test typically involves a collection of documents comprising facts and law, and you have to show your ability to analyze them and deliver legal work product. That collection may be referred to as "the library." In the library, a memorandum will set forth the task you have to perform, such as writing a memorandum of law or a letter to a client. Legal materials such as statutes, regulations, and/or cases will explain the law in your jurisdiction. Additional documents such as a newspaper article may provide additional relevant information. Often, you will have to write two practical tests, each one ninety minutes long, over the course of three hours. The practical tests count for one fifth of the bar exam grade in some jurisdictions.

Know the structure of your practical test before Exam Day. Read the instructions from published practical tests so you are familiar. Then, on Exam Day, reading the instructions should confirm what you already know, and any differences in the instructions should jump out at you. Of course, make certain you are writing your answer in the correct booklet or place.

B. Determine the Task to Be Performed

If the question calls for a memorandum, and you write a letter, that is Not A Good Thing. Accordingly, there are points to be won just by performing the proper task. When you first get to your materials (wait for permission, of course!), identify the task you are to perform. It should be near the top or the bottom of the memorandum. Be careful that you do not misinterpret something that you read quickly. "Your client received a nasty letter" does not mean that your task is to prepare a nasty letter! Circle the imperative sentence that contains your task, and make sure you set out to do that task.

C. Read the Entire Library

Next, take the time to read the entire library. Carefully read the memorandum, the statutes, cases, and regulations, and all other material in the library. Circle rules of law and pertinent bits of evidence. Ignore, for the moment, seemingly superfluous stuff like, "The defendant was very angry . . ." Plenty of superfluous stuff will appear on your first read. You may come back and use some of it, so don't ignore it completely. What if your client didn't do something he was supposed to do because the defendant was very angry, and your client reasonably feared assault or decided to de-escalate the situation? Dealing with your client's actions could change a left-the-scene-of-an-accident to a left-the-presence-of-an-angry-person-once-it-was-clear-nobody-was-severly-injured. I urge you to read every word at least once – do not skim, as you might miss something important.

If necessary, read the library a second time. This time, the entire library will be fresh in your mind (you just read it carefully).

Just like watching an awesome movie a second time, you will see things that you missed the first time. Now you have uploaded the entire library into your mental RAM, and you are ready to organize your answer.

D. All Elements Rule – Outline Your Answer

Ah, our friend, the All Elements Rule, rides again to save the day! Here the All Elements Rule requires you to go on an Easter egg hunt. Some of the elements will appear in one of the statutes, regulations, or cases you receive in your library. The rest of the elements likely will be found in the next legal document. So, for example, the first case will involve a car accident, and the court will recite the rule for negligence: "A claim of negligence requires the plaintiff to prove by a preponderance of the evidence that the defendant had a duty to the plaintiff, the defendant breached that duty, and that breach directly caused injury to the plaintiff." The second case, for example, will expound on causation, or damages. "In this jurisdiction, causation requires that the damage suffered by the plaintiff was reasonably foreseeable." Or, for example, "A plaintiff can recover for foreseeable damages, but cannot recover for special damages." So you see, it would not suffice to read the memorandum and just one legal document and start outlining your answer memo or letter.

Now you are ready to outline your answer. Our other, bestest friend, AIRAC, rides again here. Let me expand on my hypothetical above to illustrate how you might outline your answer.

MEMO

A – P wins b/c injury was foreseeable.

I – Wr. negligence lies b/c injury did not directly follow D's actions.

R – "A claim of negligence requires the plaintiff to prove by a preponderance of the evidence that the defendant had a duty to the plaintiff, the defendant breached that duty, and that breach directly caused injury to the plaintiff." AND "In this jurisdiction, causation requires that the damage suffered by the plaintiff was reasonably foreseeable."

A – All Elements – All Evidence!
C – P wins.

Notice how I copied the rule right out of the two cases.

E. Write Your Answer

Go back to the instructional memorandum in the library, and confirm that you know the task you must perform. If it is a memo, write a memo. If it is a letter, write a letter. If it is a complaint, write a complaint. To whom is the memorandum addressed? We know from whom it shall come: "Attorney at Law." Do not write your name or any identifying information, obviously. Optionally, use headings to identify the parts of your document. Be sure to answer the question. "Write a memorandum advising Mr. Green whether he could successfully sue Mr. Brown in this case." In your answer memorandum, your first sentence should be something like, "It is my legal opinion that you could successfully sue Mr. Brown on a claim of negligence in a state court of West Dakota, given the facts as I currently understand them."

Following your outline, state the issue. In many ways, your answer memorandum should feel a lot like writing an essay. (Thank you, AIRAC!) Next recite the rules. Use good legal writing protocol, such as citations. For example, "A claim of negligence requires the plaintiff to prove by a preponderance of the evidence that the defendant had a duty to the plaintiff, the defendant breached that duty, and that breach directly caused injury to the plaintiff." Smith v. Jones, 123 State Rep. 456, 460 (W.D. 2021). Yes, that's right. I just gave a citation to the first case in the library in my memorandum. Show the bar examiners that you know how to do that. Do the same for any legal authority that you quote. You do not need perfect Bluebook® citation style, but show that you get the concept of legal citation. Citation information should appear in the case somewhere.

Be certain that you address every element of the rules, especially the elements from the second case in this example, in your answer, and examine each piece of evidence in that analysis. If there are evidentiary problems, such as for example a newspaper article stating facts, indicate those problems in your answer. "The newspaper article asserts that [X] is true. Although the newspaper article itself is inadmissible in court as hearsay evidence, if admissible evidence can be developed showing that [X] is in fact true, [element C of the rule] is met in this case."

Also consider auxiliary legal issues such as jurisdiction, venue, and evidentiary burdens, where applicable. Nothing in your instructional memorandum might mention the issues of jurisdiction or venue, but if a suit could be filed in court, a real live lawyer should consider such matters. A brief sentence mentioning that the court should have personal jurisdiction over the defendant brings joy to the hearts of bar examiners everywhere.

It could come to pass that a deeper analysis is required. The cases that you are given, for example, may have relevant fact patterns that have similarities to the fact pattern that you address. If you see that, ask yourself whether the bar examiners are trying to tell you something. It may be that the examiners (or authors of the exam question) probe whether you can analyze a case, and not just discern a rule of law. "In that case, the plaintiff lost because ______. In the present case, I am confident that the plaintiff will win because [the facts differ from the prior case]." What I am talking about is diving into the facts and outcome of the cases in the library, and using similarities and differences therein to predict the outcome in your case. That's what lawyers do all the time. If you see the opportunity to do the same on the practical test, go for it!

F. All Evidence Suggestion

In the analysis portion of your answer, work hard to include all of the evidence set forth in the library. Some evidence will be revealed in the instructional memorandum, and other evidence will appear in the other documents in the library. If, at the end of your answer, you have completely left out any reference to one of the documents in the library, you are probably missing something from your answer. During the outlining, look through all of the documents at your disposal and ask yourself whether you have used something from every document. There may be multiple somethings in each document, so be thorough! This is where your thorough read will assist you to avoid missing anything. When you are completing the writing of your analysis, review whether you have addressed All of the Elements of the rules of law, and used All of the Evidence, even if, especially if, there is any evidence that goes against your conclusion.

The practical test examines less whether you can issue-spot, and examines more whether you can piece together law and facts to reach a conclusion. The library will give you complimentary rules of law from two separate documents, and Big Question Number One is whether you can use rules from those two documents in your answer. Similarly, evidence and facts appear in several documents, and Big Question Number Two is whether you can reach a sound legal conclusion based on ALL of the facts, not just those few facts that strongly support your conclusion. In your essays (see previous chapter), the bar examiners are looking for issue-spotting skills. In the practical test, the bar examiners want to see if you can handle a constellation of facts. The All Evidence Suggestion should help you consider all of the evidence, and communicate to the bar examiners that you have.

G. Manage Your Time

You should spend about thirty minutes reading the library and outlining your answer. Then spend the rest of the time writing your answer, addressing all of the elements with all of the evidence.

If organizing your answer takes more than about one-third of the time allotted, determine what is slowing you down. Is it locating the task to be performed? Is it determining the rules of law governing your task? Is it reading? If you can spot the slow step, work on that.

In my experience, reading the library takes the longest time. At first, you have a large collection of documents, initially no idea of what you are supposed to do, and the clock is ticking. Take a deep breath, and calm yourself. How do you run a marathon? One step at a time. If necessary, in practice, say aloud the act or chore you are performing, to focus your efforts. "I am looking for the rules of law that govern." Once you have read the library, it should be fairly easy to find those rules again. Importantly, do not let your mind get distracted, for example, by a key piece of evidence that you did not notice before, when you are focused on the chore of locating the rules of law. My point here is that the practical test takes discipline, rather than grand legal knowledge. Do one chore, and then do the next. Left, right, left, right, wins a marathon. As you practice, work to focus on one chore at a time. Then, work to get your organizing done in about one third of the time allotted, to leave you two-thirds of the time to write your answer.

During the DC bar exam, which included a practical test, I sat at a table with another attorney candidate. Before the practical test, she told me that she had taken the bar exam three times before. I wished her luck, and silently prayed desperately for us both, my confidence shaken. Well, I launched into the practical test, read everything, outlined my answer memorandum, and was scribbling away. Over an hour into the test, I realized that I was doing well and was perhaps a bit ahead of schedule. I paused in my writing, and I allowed my consciousness, my awareness, to expand to take in the sounds and atmosphere of the room. I was taking my first bar exam, and doing well – so far so good! Well, I did not dare take my eyes off my page, lest the exam proctor suspect I was peeking at anyone else's answer. But I could hear, all across the room, the sound of furious scribbling. Everywhere, ball point pens were scratching out memoranda explaining exactly why the client should do, or not do, something based on the law and the facts. But at my table, to my deep chagrin, I heard not the sound of scribbling, but the sound of pages flipping. "Flip, flip . .

. flip . . . flip, flip." My neighbor was flipping pages, attempting to make sense of the task at hand, and her pen was high in the air (I imagined), nowhere near the page where it might spill ink and gather points. "Here comes Number Five," I thought, with not a little sadness for my neighbor.

Incidentally, that experience fuels my writing of this book. If I can reach just one person and help them through the practical test, and enable them to put the pen on the page (or the fingers on the keyboard), maybe, just maybe, they can break on through to the other side of the bar exam, and serve our fellow citizens as an Attorney at Law . . .

Accordingly, throughout your practical test, glance at the time (and not your neighbor) to ensure that you will complete your answer on time. Work during your practice tests to leave yourself plenty of time to organize and write your answer.

H. Practice, Practice, Practice

How do you get good at practical tests? You do them! And then you look at model answers to see if you are close. At first, you might have to peek a bit at model answers, especially if the massive amount of information in the library overwhelms. But as you practice, you will see that each document in the library compliments the others, and they all fit together like a puzzle. Once you have sharpened your practical test-taking skills, you do not need to keep hammering away at them. Do a timed test or two so you get the sensation of meeting the time limit with a solid answer, and then turn to other time intensive tasks such as learning substantive law and practicing essays and multiple-choice questions. Take a practical test perhaps once or twice more as February or July lengthens. Even though the practical test may count for a quarter of your score on the bar exam, you do not need to spend one quarter of your preparation time and effort on mastering the practical test.

I. Concise Instructions for the Practical Test

Know the structure of the exam before Exam Day.

Write your answer in the correct booklet/place.

Manage your time – save 2/3 of your time for actual writing.

Identify the task to be performed.

Read the library thoroughly.

Outline your answer using AIRAC.

Confirm you are performing the correct task.

Write your answer.

Quote the rules from the library, and cite it as legal authority.

Address every element of the rules (All Elements Rule).

Use all of the evidence from the library (All Evidence Suggestion).

Use something from every document in the library.

Compare the facts and outcomes of the cases in the library with the facts of your case.

Deal with evidentiary, jurisdictional and other auxiliary issues.

V. The Multiple-Choice Part

A. A War Story

The hardest test I ever took in my life was the 1998 United States Patent Bar Examination. The pass rate barely reached 35 %, so I Am Not Kidding when I tell you it was *hard*. The exam format was rather like the multiple-choice portion of state bar exams: a hundred multiple-choice questions over six hours with a short break in between. Significantly, the exam was open book. Still, only a third of the candidates passed. Let me tell you how I did it.

I had my trusty Manual of Patent Examining Procedure on my desk, brightly flagged with sticky tongues of plastic. I favored yellow flags because pencil writing appeared with greatest contrast on the yellow portion. The "M.P.E.P." was the size of a telephone book. (If you have never seen a telephone book, ask your grandma how big that is.) And I did not *touch* the massive tome during the exam! I am sure you know that if you are diving into your book during an open-book exam, *it is too late*. I had my trusty Number Two pencils in a plastic sandwich bag, along with a small pencil sharpener. Each pencil was slightly used, because filling in a bubble on a multiple-choice test goes faster if the pencil lead tip is slightly dull. (How did I know this? Practice tests!) Those pencils became my lucky talisman on all future bar exams, and I have lent them to others for their bar exams, LSAT tests, SAT and ASVAB tests. The repeated successes add to the pencil's mystical powers. Sitting here today, I can still smell the woody aroma of those pencils ready to take that exam.

The exam was difficult to say the least. I battled through the first half that morning, and ate my sandwich with friends at lunch. Our nervous banter gave way to the afternoon struggle. I slogged through grueling questions for almost three more hours to reach the home stretch. Ten minutes were left, and a dozen questions remained untouched. I turned the page, and to my surprise, the fact pattern for the next question was *massive*. Most questions were about two thirds of a column long, and two questions appeared on a page. But not this behemoth! It sprawled all the way down the first column, and half-way down the second. I flipped the page. Another monster! I flipped more pages, and there were *five beastly questions in a row!* Mercifully, I found the last few questions were of average length. I dove into those questions, blasting through the short fact patterns and selecting the best answers my tired brain could seize. I was *very careful* to mark the answer bubble on my answer sheet next to the number of the question I was answering. Two minutes remained. I turned back to the five massive questions.

My blood ran cold. There was no way I could even *read* one fact pattern in the time left. I scanned the answers, and Answer E stated "All of the above," indicating that Answers A, B, C, and D were all correct answers to the question. With fatalistic calm washing over me, I marked "E." I had nothing to lose, and there was no way I could discern a better answer before time was up. I turned the page. Answer E for the next question was "None of the above." I furiously marked E with my very-dull pencil. Turned the page. Answer E said something about "...the above." Answer E got filled in. Flip! I noted the word "above" in the brief answer next to the letter E, so again I marked "E." The final monster fact pattern emerged into view on the next page, and I marked Answer E before even noticing that Answer E related to the "above" Answers A through D. "Time!" bellowed the proctor, and my pencil rose from the page. My hand trembled ever so slightly, and my weary eyes regarded the string of black pearls down the "E" column on my answer sheet. I was done.

Because I had completed a number of practice exams beforehand, I estimated that I scored right around 70 % on the real exam. And passing required 70 %, so I was on pins and needles wondering if I would have to take the bastard again.

Months later, the answers were published, and I learned I had passed. Many friends were not so fortunate (I worked in a large patent law firm then, and we newbies all studied for it together). I tore through the answers and found that **ONE** of the monster questions had a correct answer of E. I warmed with satisfaction, knowing that my desperate grab at Answer E got me one more correct answer. And to this day, I am sure that single correct answer put me over the top to pass the Hardest Test I Ever Took.

B. Studying for a Multiple-Choice Exam

In my view, studying for a multiple-choice test requires almost more practice than internalization. But it does require internalization. Besides, each subject on the multiple-choice exam appears on the essay exam, and could appear in the practical test. So do not forget your internalization.

Briefly, do the same things to internalize, to study, for a multiple-choice test as you would do for the essay exam. Outline, or prepare flash cards, or whatever works for you.

C. Practicing for a Multiple-Choice Exam

Honestly, though, by far the most effective way to study for the multiple-choice portion of the bar exam is to read a practice question, struggle to identify the correct answer, and then look up the correct answer. Go back to the question and reason out why the right answer is the right answer. Early in your approach to a new subject, also look up the black letter law that governs the question.

Patterns will emerge. You will read a question, and intuitively you will begin to sense the call of the question. What are they looking for? If you do enough practice questions, you will become very good at recognizing those patterns. And, a bonus effect will be enjoyed on Exam Day: You will see the *same questions* again! It is very easy to struggle with a question before the exam, learn the right answer and why, and then see the same question again. Easy points! But always read the question very carefully! A "not" changes the question 180 degrees, as does a change from "The defendant is *guilty* because . . ." to "The defendant is *acquitted* because . . .." I saw substantially the same question maybe one-in-twenty questions, because I did **a lot** of practice questions (you should too!).

Here's how to attack a multiple-choice question:

Read the question (not the fact pattern) first, to know what the question seeks.
Read, or skim, the answer choices to know what the answer will look like.
Read the fact pattern carefully.
Read the question again.
Read the answer choices carefully.
Eliminate the two wrong answers.
Make the best choice between the two remaining answers.
Mark the answer on the question AND on the answer sheet.

Okay, let's work through an example.

> Johnny was walking his pet lion, named Leo, down the sidewalk one day. He had the lion on a leash, and

carried with him an electric stun gun. Johnny and Leo encountered George walking toward them on the sidewalk. When George saw Johnny and Leo, George continued walking toward them and did not cross the street. Leo suddenly escaped Johnny's control and attacked George. Johnny was unable to control Leo or stop the attack even using the stun gun on Leo. Leo bit George, causing injury.

Johnny is liable to George for his injury caused by Leo because:

A. Johnny failed to act as a holder in due course in controlling Leo.

B. George was not contributorily negligent.

C. Leo violated George's Fourth Amendment rights.

D. Johnny is strictly liable.

First, read the question. That is the sentence (or fragment thereof) right before the lettered answer choices. "Johnny is liable to George for his injury caused by Leo because:" That tells you a wealth of information. We are looking for a reason to find Johnny liable. Someone (something) named Leo did the injury, and someone named George got the worst of it. Incidentally, the question further informs you this is probably a torts question because of the words "liable" and "injury." Now skim the answers. Answer A is probably not the right answer, because "holder in due course" is not a tort doctrine. If you are confident that A is a ridiculous choice, put a light pencil mark through "A," so you do not waste time reading Answer A again. Answer B looks good, because contributory negligence is a tort doctrine. Answer C looks ridiculous because the Fourth Amendment does not relate to tort liability. But keep an open mind – we haven't read the fact pattern yet. (What if Leo is a police dog, and Johnny a cop?) Answer D looks good right now, at least because strict liability also is a tort theory.

Now read the fact pattern carefully. (I will pause while you read.) Okay, we got a pet lion, Johnny the owner, George the victim. Johnny took all those precautions to control the lion, namely the leash and the stun gun, but the lion still attacked. Read the question again carefully. Johnny is liable. Why? Read the answer choices carefully. There was no unlawful search and seizure, so Answer C can be crossed off for sure now. Answer A remains ridiculous, too, although now you see the humor – Johnny was holding the leash, but that did not make him a holder in due course. Light pencil marks through "A" and "C" indicate that you have eliminated the two wrong answers.

Now you have to pick between Answer B and Answer D. This is where the question separates Attorneys at Law from People Who Just Watch Court TV. Answer B says that George was not contributorily negligent. Note in the fact pattern that "George continued walking toward them and did not cross the street." (Hey, if I saw a lion walking toward me, even if he was on a leash, I am not sure I would just keep walking Right Into The Jaws Of Death! Reasonable people find a way to avoid the lion, right?) But George had every right to be on the sidewalk. He pays his taxes (we may presume), and could reasonably assume that someone walking a lion on a sidewalk would have control over the big cat. So Answer B looks pretty good, right? But Answer B is incorrect.

Answer D is correct because you previously read, outlined, or flashcarded the rule that "exotic or wild animals carry strict liability for their owners." Or you learn it when you look up the right answer to the question. It matters not whether Johnny was negligent when strict liability controls. If Johnny's negligence does not come into play, George's *contributory negligence* is irrelevant as well. Answer D is the best choice as between Answer B and Answer D, therefore.

Put a dash next to Answer B and circle Answer D. Do this so that you can be certain that you have marked your answer next to the right number on your answer sheet. Also, the dash tells you that Answer B was the Least Ridiculous Answer among the wrong answers, if you have time to come back and review the question. You could evaluate whether Answer B or Answer

D is correct, if you still have doubt. More good practices appear below.

D. Good Test Taking Practices

There are many beautiful things about a multiple-choice test. First, the right answer is already on the page. Second, if you have no clue about a question, it is just one teeny tiny little question on a great big exam. You don't even have to answer that question and you will still pass the bar exam. Third, when you complete the multiple-choice portion of the bar exam, you are done! No more pencils, no more books, no more bar examiner's dirty looks!

During the test, note the start time so you can gauge the end time. It can make a huge difference if the test started at 9:00 AM or 9:10 AM. That knowledge will mean a lot to you at about 11:55 AM, and you have eight questions left. Do you have just five minutes left in the test? Or are you aware that you have fifteen minutes, until 12:10 PM?

Mark your answers in your test booklet. Use a system, so you know what your marks mean. Above, I suggested crossing out the letters of the ridiculous answers, or the answers you know are wrong. Put a dash next to the least ridiculous answer, and circle the letter of the answer you determine to be correct. Circling the correct answer will save your mind, heart, general overall health, and your Lawyer Candidacy when you glance back from time to time to ensure that you are marking the answers next to the correct numbers on the answer sheet. Be careful to avoid any appearance of cheating. Shield your test booklet (and your answer sheet) so your fellow attorney candidates cannot see your answers. Avoid any appearance of impropriety. You do not want to have to explain your innocence when the exam proctor catches your neighbor repeatedly looking your way.

Mark your answers clearly on your answer sheet. Start with a slightly-dull pencil, and fill in the bubble completely. Do not place incomplete marks on your answer sheet with the idea that you will come back to fill in the bubbles. (What if they call time before you fill in those bubbles?) Fill in each bubble *as you go*. It is a correct answer in the bag, and you never have to mess with it again.

Mark your answer next to the correct number. Seriously. I have heard sob stories where people taking multiple-choice tests skipped a line, or placed two answers on the same line, and then every subsequent answer appeared next to an incorrect number. *The horror!* Freak out about this now. (I will pause while you freak out.) But don't make that mistake on Exam Day!

I offer two techniques for avoiding marking the answer next to the wrong number.

First, circle your answer in your test booklet. Then, from time to time, spot-check your answer sheet. "Question 27 – I marked 'A' in my test booklet. On my answer sheet, next to '27,' I see 'A' marked." Do that once every ten or thirty minutes. If you do The Bad, Bad Thing, do not panic.

Your answers are circled in your test booklet, so you can readily find where your answer sheet got off track and fix it. It is worth the few minutes it would take to correct your answer sheet, because you already worked hard to cipher the correct answers. Now go get credit for them! The question or two you might have to skip later in the test, just guess at an answer if you must.

Second, when you determine the correct answer, say to yourself the question number AND the correct answer. "47 is B." Then, place your finger on "47" on your answer sheet, and fill in bubble "B." Repeat to yourself, "47 is B." Then look back at your test booklet on your way to Question 48, and confirm that for Question 47, you have circled Answer B. "Yep. 47 is B." Of course, do NOT use your outside-your-head voice when doing that.

Mark an answer for every question. As you can see in my War Story above, it got me another point, even though I had no hope of comprehending the question in the time I had left. As you keep track of your time, note when you have only a few minutes left. Then pick a letter and mark away for every unanswered question you have left. I think it is best to pick just one letter, than to randomly mark letters. If you go with one letter, chances are decent that you will get every one-in-four correct. I favor the letter "C." I picked Answer E on the Patent Bar Exam just because of the "all of the above," "none of the above" format of Answer E for those monster questions.

Circle, or place a star or other mark, in your test booklet next to the number of the questions that trouble you. Then, if you finish with time left, go back through your test booklet looking for those trouble questions. Attack the question again, and see if you calmly and rationally arrive at a different answer. If you remain unsure, and cannot pick between the two best answers, leave the question and move on. Or, if you become certain of one answer, mark your answer sheet accordingly.

If you finish with time left, look at your answer sheet. Have you answered every question? Have you filled in the right bubbles completely? Spot check against your test booklet to ensure that the circled answers are marked on your answer sheet. Erase fully any answers that you marked and then changed. Also erase completely any stray pencil marks on your answer sheet. Make sure your identification appears filled in correctly on your answer sheet. Now smile, Counselor: **You have finished the bar exam!**

VI. What to Expect on Exam Day

A. To Write, or to Type?

Back in my day (insert geezer cough here), the vast majority of attorney candidates wrote the essays by hand. However, we had a choice whether we would write the bar exam essays by hand, or type it out on our laptops. Those who applied and were allowed to type their essays were placed in a separate room so that the deafening sound of their fingers pounding away on keyboards would not distract those of us furiously scribbling. (A thousand people scribbling can form a pretty impressive sound, too.)

If you strongly prefer one format over the other, pay attention to how and when you must select your desired format. You may have to request that format as early as when you first apply to sit for the bar exam. If you want to type, make sure that you refresh your laptop with any necessary software updates, you have properly downloaded the software for the bar exam, and your laptop functions perfectly. The exam proctors will be sympathetic to you on Exam Day if you are having a malfunction, but they might not have the time or the talent to sort out why your laptop does not want to cooperate. Be prepared to write out your essays as a Back-Up Plan.

The software the bar will ask you to download isolates your screen from the rest of your laptop's memory and storage to prevent cheating. That software allows you to type up your essays and submit them in a secure, identifiable way, while making anything else stored on your laptop inaccessible while the exam software runs. Even so, avoid having anything on your laptop on Exam Day that could be misconstrued as material useful for cheating. You just do not want to have to explain why your secured transactions outline rests undeleted in your Recycle Bin. Avoid the appearance of impropriety.

If you decide to write your essays by hand, select a useful pen. To do that, I purchased booklets containing the same relatively flimsy paper that the actual exam booklets would contain, and I tested a number of pens on that paper. I tested which pens wrote well, and which pens' ink did not bleed through the paper. I favored Pilot V-Ball pens with "fine" tips (0.5 mm) and blue ink. "Medium" tips (0.7 mm) and "wide" tips (1.0 mm) bled through – I saved those luxurious ink bleeders for signing my name to all those lawyer letters I was going to write after I passed the bar. When practicing, use actual booklets at least once to familiarize yourself with size limitations and mechanics of writing in those booklets.

Write double space. Leave a space in between your writing. This does a couple of things. First, and very importantly, it makes your essay easier to read. It may even improve your handwriting. Second, it gives you a chance to insert a sentence. In my experience, bar examiners do not mind the occasional additional thought. However, if your whole essay appears chaotically disorganized, that is Not A Good Thing.

Write legibly. Practice, and make the effort to really make each word legible. Some abbreviations are okay, but do not write your essay with the same grammar with which you text your friends. (I recall vividly Prof. Freer warning us in his Bar/Bri® lecture on civil procedure to spell out the word "question" in lieu of a question mark as an abbreviation, so the bar examiners do not read your issue statement as, "This is a federal?")

Practice should help you decide whether to write or to type. (Do this before it is too late to change your choice with the bar!) If you write illegibly, then type. If you type way too slowly, then write! Let me teach you a hint about typing, if you never took a typing class: the "F" key and the "J" key have little ridges on them so you can re-orient your hands without looking at the keyboard. (As I type that, I have to admit that I do not use those ridges. Instead, I look at the screen and use that to orient my hands. If I type gibberish, my fingers are hitting the wrong keys.)

B. Travel to the Bar Exam

Woody Allen said 80 % of life is showing up. Someone else said, "99 % of life is showing up *prepared*." Fair enough. I say, "100 % of the people who pass the bar exam show up *well practiced*." I digress. Please show up to the bar exam. I urge you to secure hotel accommodations in the town where the exam will take place long before the exam itself. Everybody and their grandmother will also stay in town those days. Get a hotel room as close to the exam venue as possible, hopefully so you can walk, especially if parking will be problematic. If you must drive, reduce your keys to the bare essentials. You don't want that fancy key fob to raise suspicions. I am serious.

Get to town at least a day early, two if you can swing it. Acclimatize yourself to your room, the town, the weather. Award yourself bonus points if someone else will drive you, if driving is necessary. You can continue to study along the way, or rest, even if you are not asleep.

On Exam Day, get there reasonably early. You do not want the stress of traffic to damage the aura of prepared confidence that you will exude that morning. It is better to arrive early, get registered, and get seated than to have to run in late and risk the exam proctors telling you to go home because the exam has already begun.

C. Sleep, Nutrition, and Hydration

I know the bar exam represents, shall we say, an exciting time. Your desire to cram it all in may tempt you to cut back or skip sleep. This is not a law school fun run one-hour exam that you could cram for the night before. You must take care of your body and your mind, and be prepared to endure two or three days of testing. That requires sleep.

I would urge you to avoid drugs, especially drugs that you have not used before or don't use regularly. No, I don't mean heroin and cocaine drugs. I mean caffeine and sleep aids. If you do not know how your body will react, the night before Exam Day is no time to experiment. Being too juiced on caffeine or too groggy from a sleeping pill might throw you off your game. For a mild stimulant, go for a walk or a run. To sleep better at night, go for a walk or run early the day before. Having said that, if you have a coffee habit, for example, please by all means continue. Just don't overdo it. The adrenaline will carry you pretty far anyway.

As Exam Day gets closer, regulate your nutrition and hydration to give you three-hour periods each morning and each afternoon where you do not need food, water, or a bathroom break. Train your body by blocking out those times from 9:00 AM to noon, and from 1:00 PM to 4:00 PM, and avoiding sustenance during those times. Practice also eating a light lunch only, so that you do not have food coma during the afternoon.

I believe that one of my four bar exams allowed us to bring a bottle of water. I cannot recall which one. Was it South Carolina? We had nicely air-conditioned rooms at the state fairgrounds in Columbia. Was it Virginia? Could have been. We took the test in a large ballroom of a fancy hotel in Richmond. I am pretty sure it was not allowed for the DC bar exam. There, the test was administered in several rooms of a public library or a school – funny how I can't recall exactly. (That's what I want for you: that the Bar Exam is a vague contented memory in your distant past!) I remember the patent bar exam allowed us to bring a sandwich in a clear sandwich bag, but we could not touch it until lunchtime. In any case, know exactly what you are allowed to bring in the way of snacks and beverages, and train your body to conform to what you can bring in the week or so leading up to Exam Day.

D. What You Can Bring; What You Cannot Bring

You can bring only what the bar says you can bring. Read those instructions carefully, and do not goof it up. Anything that you bring that is not allowed, be ready to trash it or put it in your car during the exam. Make sure your laptop is fully charged; the exam proctors may provide an electrical outlet for you to charge your laptop during the exam.

Definitely bring pens and pencils (sharpened, but slightly dull). Bring your laptop preloaded with the software for taking the bar exam. The Virginia bar examiners insisted that everything we brought fit into a clear sandwich bag (except for the laptop), so our full possessions could be readily examined for contraband. That list included: an identification, a registration document, six pens, six pencils, and keys. An analogue watch. Oh yeah, medication if you had a doctor's note and cleared it ahead of time. Whew. That's it.

The Virginia bar exam also required us to dress like lawyers – suits and ties for the guys, equivalent for the girls – but also insisted on soft-soled shoes so you wouldn't disturb others if you had to get up and walk around. Imagine a thousand attorney candidates in suits, dresses, and tennis shoes! My point: know your dress code, if there is one, for the bar exam.

E. Watch Your Time, and Follow Directions

I know I have said it before, but it is worth saying it again. Attorney candidates, smart people, get defeated on the bar exam by simple mechanics. They skip a multiple-choice question, and then complete an entire column of questions before they realize that they are marking their answers on the wrong row. And they are unable to see where they began this awful mistake. The whole answer sheet becomes suspect. Or, in their haste, they have written the family law essay in the secured transactions answer booklet. Because the booklet does not mention "holder in due course" anywhere, the bar examiner cannot award a single point. *And watch your time.* I am sure you can write a better answer if you have an hour per question; unfortunately, you only have thirty minutes.

Following directions also means avoiding disqualification. Make certain that you give the exam proctors no reason to throw you out of the bar exam, or to suspect you of cheating. Don't open your packet until they tell you to. Don't flip over the fact pattern until they tell you to. The exam proctors are not brutal horrible people, but if you cannot follow their instructions, they have no choice but to act accordingly. Further, they cannot let one attorney candidate disrupt the bar exam for all of the other candidates. I have seen it where someone opened the packet too soon – the exam proctors corrected the candidate and the candidate rapidly flipped over the documents so nothing could be read. It was clear to all that nerves, and not mischievous intent, caused the packet to open early, so the candidate suffered no other consequence. Finally, stop when time is called. If you have a chance, put a period on the page as your pen lifts in the air – like you meant to end it that way! Seeking one more point is not worth risking total disqualification.

VII. Final Word of Encouragement

Remember, Dear Reader, this is a marathon, not a sprint. It is a marathon both in the sense that you have a lot of work to do in the next two months, and in the sense that two or three days of testing will require stamina and endurance. Accordingly, you need to take care of yourself mentally and physically. And emotionally and spiritually, for that matter. Let's talk physical. You must eat right, with a variety of foods in sufficient amount. Sure, indulge a little with junk food and caffeine if you like (I hit some coffee ice cream when I was studying for my first bar exam – how's that for killing two birds with one stone!). Avoid stress eating, though. You must get sufficient sleep, of course. I strongly urge you to exercise in accordance with your current state of fitness. Walking or running gets you some fresh air and keeps your metabolism going. Go for a walk once a day and/or a run every other day (of course, after you have consulted with your fave health care provider). Exercise releases endorphins that give you a sense of well-being, so use that to combat negative feelings during your preparation. Keep in touch with your significant other, your mom, your dad, your besties, your classmates, whomever, to provide you that emotional grounding. *You can do this,* and they can help. Study groups also help, but use them to encourage one another, and do not let them devolve into freak-out sessions, nor let them distract you from studying with a false sense of effective effort. Exchange and constructively critique practice essays and practical test answers. Stay spiritually nurtured too. I have heard it said that prayer will never be abolished from public schools until they do away with pop quizzes. And so it is among attorney candidates so long as there are bar exams. Praise the Lord and pass the Number Two pencils!

If you have any feedback, war stories, criticisms, or victory speeches, please e-mail me at DrStipkala@gmail.com. And I really want to hear your victory speech, Counselor! What helped you pass the bar exam? What did not help so much? How can we help future attorney candidates enjoy a more effective bar exam preparation experience? I ask for your feedback because being a lawyer is really about helping others, serving others. As your First Act as a Successful Attorney candidate and Conqueror Of The Bar Exam, help me help others with your feedback. I and they would be most grateful!

Perspectives on Passing the Bar Exam: How We Did It, and How You Can, Too!

By

Peter L. Brewer, Esq.
Sabrina C. Call, Esq.
Bernard S. Klosowski, Jr., Esq.
John M. Rappold, Esq.,
and
Jeremy M. Stipkala, Esq.

To you, Dear Reader:
May You Pass The Bar Exam!

Table of Contents

I. Jeremy's Introduction

Here we go, Dear Reader! It is time to start studying for the bar exam!

You are probably flush with joyful confidence as you graduate from law school: you have mastered a new, practical, prestigious, stimulating, and wonderful area of human knowledge and endeavor, **The Law**. Yet that confidence is tinged with a shadow of anxiety about the upcoming bar exam. If you do not pass the bar exam, all you will have is a nice diploma to hang on the wall and so much legal knowledge that makes you a walking civics course. Oh yeah, and a ton of student debt. If you think about it too much, that anxiety will blossom into raw fear and ruin your day. At the furthest periphery of your mind lurks the awful question that no-one dares whisper aloud, *"What if I do not pass the bar exam?"*

Fear not, Dear Reader! On the pages that follow, a diverse group of attorneys relate their bar exam experiences. They range from those who passed on the first try, to those who needed multiple attempts and endured *years* of that anxious question gnawing at their minds. We have attorneys who took bar exams in multiple jurisdictions, and another who can compare The Old Format with the Uniform Bar Exam. Each attorney prepared for the bar exam differently. Some attorneys studied full-time, while others studied while working a job. Significantly, we believe that the life circumstances surrounding our bar exam success stories will resonate with different segments of our audience. That's you, Dear Reader. We have captured here what each of those attorneys, if they could jump into a time machine, would tell their younger selves about **what worked for them to pass the bar exam.**

We sincerely hope that you find much that is useful. Significantly, we wrote this book for two kinds of attorney candidates: those who want to pass on their **first attempt**, and those who want to pass on their *very next* attempt. Several wonderful bar preparation courses teach the substance of the law tested on the bar exam. However, given the *thousands and thousands* of attorney candidates who fail each year, there must be something missing from those attorney candidates' preparation. We offer our insight with the aspiration that you, Dear Reader, *do not have to take the bar exam again.*

This diverse group of attorneys has two things in common. First, we all passed the bar exam. Second, we each care very deeply about the attorney candidates who follow in our footsteps. So please read on. We look forward to you joining us in that extraordinarily marvelous endeavor, **the licensed practice of law**.

II. Peter's Thoughts on Passing the Bar Examination

By Peter L. Brewer, Esq.

A. "Absolutely American"

Several years ago, I read a book called "Absolutely American." The book was written by a Rolling Stones writer, and followed students at West Point as they moved through the process of becoming commissioned officers. The writer was granted unusual access to the military academy, and was able to interview and follow individual students during their careers at West Point. One thing that stood out to me was that every cadet had his or her own unique motivation for going through the grueling process.

For many their motivation was pure patriotism – they wanted to become Rangers or they wanted to fly helicopters or they wanted to be in the Corps of Engineers

– they wanted to serve. For others, it was the opportunity for a free education, and little more. For others, it was a stepping stone for a later career on Wall Street or in business. Whatever the driving force, the ones who made it through were the ones who kept their focus on the end goal without getting discouraged by the endless challenges and obstacles presented at West Point.

One of those challenges is that each cadet is intentionally given more tasks each day than they can handle, or at least excel at. This means that each cadet has to make a decision daily as to what is most important, knowing that many other things must receive less attention.

B. What Is Most Important?

The bar examination is the same way. Regardless of their motive for wanting to become a lawyer, the law school graduate must create a plan and stick to it. He or she must decide each day, based on the plan, what is most important for that day. One can only spend so much time on criminal procedure, knowing that there are many other topics that need to be addressed. Therefore, my advice is to read what you can, memorize what you can, and move on. Do not succumb to the temptation of going back and studying yesterday's outlines and notes, because then you will miss today's information.

Studying for the bar exam is like eating an elephant – it can be eaten only one bite at a time. The amount of material is overwhelming, but if you plan your time in advance, you can take those bites in manageable quantities, and perhaps even come back to chew those same bites again right before the test. Stay focused on the ultimate goal, and do not let yourself become discouraged because you can't master it all.

We have all heard stories of individuals who went to law school, then took the bar exam, and failed. And they took the exam a second time and still did not pass. There are two reasons for this – either they did not establish a base of legal knowledge while they were in law school, and now it is simply too late, or they did establish a proper base but they did not respect the test enough to adequately study before sitting for the bar. Assuming that you actually attended classes in law school and made an effort to learn the material, you should have acquired the knowledge and skills needed to pass the bar, and pass it the first time. Now you have to create the time – two to three months of your life – and dedicate yourself to intense daily study.

You must create a calendar setting out what you will study each day. Follow the calendar, read the outlines, and make outlines of the outlines. In this digital world there is still no better way to learn material than to write it down. And once you have done that, trust your instincts; trust your base of knowledge you have; and trust your ability to recall information. You will do fine.

Do not be lulled into a false sense of security based on your performance in law school. I know a law review editor that failed the first time, and I know people who were at the bottom of their law school class who did very well taking the bar. The key, again, is respecting the test and studying daily.

C. "How Do You Spell That Name Again?"

My first year out of law school I was fortunate enough to be selected to serve as a Brief Attorney at the Texas Supreme Court. One of the jobs of the supreme court is to oversee the Board of Law Examiners in Texas, and to "bless" the results of the examination when they come in. This also means that the very first people to actually see the test results and to know who passed are the staff working at the court. Law school graduates know this and make it a point to find out who the Briefing Attorneys are going in.

Shortly after the test results came in, the phones in my office started ringing. It was my friends, and friends of my friends, and even people I did not know, calling in to ask, "Is my name on the list?" It was always a joy to tell someone that they had passed and that their years of hard work had paid off. (I confess that it was also a joy to toy with them by asking them to spell their name several times, and dragging out my "search process" by a few extra moments.) But it was terribly difficult to tell someone that their name was not found, and they will have to try again, or maybe there was an administrative issue that just needs to be remedied.

You know the statistics – you know that most students pass on the first try. If you respect the test and study diligently, disciplining yourself to follow your calendar as you go, your odds are very high that you will be fine.

III. How Sabrina Studied for and Passed the South Carolina Bar Exam

By Sabrina C. Call, Esq.

A. Introduction

During law school I knew eventually I would have to take the bar exam, but it was not something I was worried about in the least. At that time, I was solely focused on the classes I was taking and the exams I had to pass in order to graduate from law school. I just assumed passing the bar exam would happen magically after graduating, and I would move into the next phase of my life. My lackadaisical attitude is one of the big reasons why I did not pass the bar exam on my first try. Let me paint a picture for you of my first attempt.

In January 2014, I was in my 3L year of law school and I had just started working a new part-time job. On top of that, I got engaged on New Year's Eve. So, newly engaged and employed, I was thrilled with the way life was going. I was counting down the days until I would graduate and finally enter the "real world."

A few weeks after graduating in May 2014, I began studying for the July bar exam using a nationally recognized bar prep course online. I had signed up for this bar prep course at the beginning of my 1L year. I remember these companies had tables set up in our library advertising their services. If I signed up for the course, I could pay a portion of the cost each year during law school instead of paying for the whole thing at the end. It sounded like a great plan to me, so I signed up.

Once I was nearing the home stretch of law school, my professors and bar prep advisors all recommended that students STOP working if we had a job, postpone planning anything big like a wedding (my fiancé and I had decided to get married in September, a mere six weeks after the bar exam), and treat studying as a full-time job. I did the exact opposite.

I decided to keep my part-time job so I would have at least a little bit of money coming in and I knew I would be glad to have the job once the bar exam was over. When I wasn't working, I was studying at home. The bar prep course I had chosen provided me with a schedule to follow from May through July. Each day would focus on a specific topic, and they spelled out exactly what I should try to accomplish each day in order to cover all of the material by exam day.

This all sounds well and good, but in reality, the daily expectations for this course seemed outrageous. I had already fallen behind after the first few days. I tried telling myself that maybe that was normal. Maybe the expectations for this course were purposely set higher than necessary just to motivate people and keep them feeling a sense of urgency. I had heard from other bar studiers that "no one" was able to keep up with the course expectations, so that helped me feel okay with my progress.

B. Study Techniques for Bar Exam Number One

The study materials included with my bar prep course included online video lectures for all of the different subjects with a handy fill-in-the-blank book to use as you watched the lectures. This book was actually very helpful and helped me stay focused as I watched the lectures.

I did have the option of going to a classroom each day with other bar studiers, but this option did not suit me at all. I tried this method one day and then never went back. The day I arrived I saw a classroom full of people in my same situation. After a few minutes someone came in and pushed "play" on the lecture video. I was a bit baffled. What was the point in me driving downtown to watch a video when I could stay at home and watch the same video? At home, I could press pause, I could rewind the video if I ever missed something, or I could take a break and eat if I got hungry. There seemed to be no benefit to me sitting in a classroom while watching the video lecture, so I was done with that.

Along with the video lectures, my study materials also included countless practice essays, countless practice MBE questions and numerous practice exams of various lengths.

I remember I watched all of the video lectures, even the ones that were painstakingly boring. I completed some of the practice MBE questions, some of the practice essays and a couple of the full-length practice exams. I do not remember the number of essays or questions available to me, but I can assure you I did not complete all of them. I also did not keep track of the number of practice MBE questions I completed, nor did I keep track of the number of essays or practice exams I completed. I was unbelievably slack with my studying. Mentally I still did not appreciate how difficult the bar exam was going to be.

I do, however, remember buying nearly a million white index cards. I spent hours upon hours creating flash cards, and I guarantee I spent 90% more time making the flash cards than actually using them. I told myself that making them was good practice since I had to read the law and write it out, but this was a terrible plan for me. If you can make flash cards quickly in the beginning, and then actually use them to study during the couple of months leading up to the exam, then by all means go right ahead. It may be helpful for you, but the way I did it was not. I'm pretty sure I was just trying to distract myself, subconsciously, from actually having to study.

C. Distractions, Distractions

I am not blaming her, let me just get that out of the way. But on top of everything my Mom called, texted or emailed me just about every day. She would think of things that needed to be done to prepare for the wedding (coming up in September) and wanted to discuss them with me. This is completely normal, but I really wasn't interested in planning the wedding. I wanted to get married, but I just wanted someone to tell me when to show up and I would be there. My Mom's stress about the wedding did not help my state of mind for studying.

If I could go back in time, obviously I would not turn down the proposal. My husband and I were destined to be together. I wouldn't change the time of year we got married either. The only thing I would do differently would be to skip taking that first July bar exam. It was a complete waste of my time, money and energy since I was trying to juggle too many things at once and I did not give the bar exam the attention and priority that it deserved.

If I had waited until after our wedding, I could have applied for the February bar exam and had one less (huge) thing on my plate while studying. Throughout law school, it was always my plan to graduate and then take the exam. It never occurred to me to postpone taking the bar exam. If I had waited, another six months would have gone by and I still wouldn't be an attorney. Being impatient is part of my personality, so that is unfortunately not something that I could change.

My Advice Tip #1 – If you have too many things going on in your life when you are planning to take the bar exam, JUST WAIT. There will be another chance for you to take the exam in a few months, so be patient.

D. Marathon Training

Another thing you cannot fully appreciate until you've taken the bar exam is the physical toll this exam will take on your body. This cannot be understated. You obviously have to train your mind to be prepared for the exam of a lifetime, but if you aren't physically prepared as well, then you really will start to notice it after the first section or two of the exam. It sounds weak to complain about sitting in a chair for three days, but your body isn't used to it so you need to train your body and increase your stamina and endurance.

To prepare, you have to make yourself get exercise while you are studying and eat healthy. Figure out a routine that works for you. I've always preferred exercising first thing in the morning, so that's what I did. After studying for hours, if I needed a break I would go for a walk outside or go swimming to get some more exercise and sunshine. Having a head full of legal knowledge is great, but if your body starts to feel drained and tired, then you are not going to be able to recall all of that knowledge when you need it the most during the exam. It truly is like training for a marathon, mentally and physically.

E. Location, Location, Location

The South Carolina bar exam is held two times each year in Columbia, South Carolina. Columbia is my home town, so I stayed at my Mom's house during my first bar exam instead of getting a hotel room. Each of the three exam mornings I would get up, drive downtown, find a parking spot in the garage and go inside to take the exam.

After the exam each day I would drive the twenty minutes back to my Mom's house and eat dinner with my family. I do not remember studying much, if at all, after the exam because all of my energy was completely drained. Staying with my Mom seemed like the most logical plan. At the time, it didn't make sense for me to get a hotel room when I had a perfectly good room waiting at my Mom's house. When that first bar exam was finally over, I had no idea if I had done well or not. I had no feeling of confidence or impending doom. Everything just felt like a blur and mentally, and probably physically, I had my fingers crossed.

I failed this first exam, and afterwards I decided I had to do things completely differently for my second attempt. That following February I stayed in a hotel right across from the Convention Center where the bar exam is held. This time I still went out to eat with my family each night after each day of the exam, but I did review some of the study materials at the end of each day. Doing away with that morning commute did relieve some of my stress. Being able to sleep an extra ten minutes and then just walk across the street for the exam was great. I highly recommend getting a hotel room to anyone who is planning to take the bar exam. And make sure to book it early, because the hotels will fill up quickly.

After failing my second exam, I knew I had to change things drastically for my third attempt. That following July, for my third bar exam attempt, I stayed in a hotel across from the Convention Center again, but this time I did not see my family while I was in town. I hibernated in my room, I ate dinner in my room and I studied the whole time when I wasn't taking the exam. I was constantly reviewing notes or study material and I was totally in the zone this time. And it worked!

F. Pulling Yourself Together After Failing

When the bar exam is over, you feel a bit of relief, but then you realize you have to wait two or three months before the results are released. You have to get back on track in the real world, whether you want to or not. Just because you've been in bar prep mode does not mean your bills stop coming.

After each bar exam, I immediately went looking for a new job. After the first bar exam, I was fortunate and found a full-time job as a legal assistant with a local law firm that needed my help "at least through the end of November." They were preparing for a murder trial, and needed someone who could stay with the firm at least through the end of the trial. I wasn't planning to go into criminal law as a career, but this sounded like a really great opportunity to me since I needed to be working, but would hopefully pass the bar exam in a few months and then be looking for a full-time attorney position in a different field.

Everything was going well until October when I learned I had not passed the bar exam. I was at work when I got the results, and I could not have been more devastated.

My Advice Tip #2 – Do not get the bar exam results while you are at work, if you can help it. If you don't pass, you will feel devastated and you won't want to be around other people. I wish I could have been at home when the results were posted.

I'm sure many people, after they learn they haven't passed, will want to drink themselves into oblivion. That is somewhat understandable, but I didn't do that. I probably had a drink that night, but nothing remarkable. I knew, as devastated as I was, that my next step would be to STOP WORKING, completely this time, and study full-time for the February bar exam. I was worried about what my husband was going to think about my plan. I hated to tell him I was going to be putting my life on pause for the next three months and not bringing any money in, but I knew I had to be selfish about this. Luckily my husband was very understanding. So, I worked a few more weeks at my job and then left on good terms. I ordered my next round of study materials, applied for the February bar exam, and started studying.

I did not pass the second exam either, but I was much, much closer. When the second exam was over, I knew I needed to find another job. This time I worked for a really wonderful financial institution in town. I have amazing memories from that job, and

I still keep in touch with the people I met there. I have even received client referrals from this company. For many reasons, I count that experience as one of the best in my life.

When the exam results came out a few months later, I learned again that I had not passed the bar exam. I had improved by leaps and bounds, though, and was much closer to passing. This time I planned ahead and was at home when I got my results, just to be on the safe side.

I hated to think I had to stop working again, but that's what I did. I stopped working and focused full time, again, on studying for my third bar exam.

G. What Worked for My Preparation?

My efforts preparing for my third and final bar exam were different than in the past. This time I kept track of every single thing I was doing. I answered over 2000 MBE prep questions, which I believe was the key to me passing the MBE. That seemed to be the magic number because at that point I felt like that the questions start repeating themselves in different ways, and my brain already had most of them memorized. This is the frame of mind you want to be in when you head in to take the MBE. Your brain should almost be on autopilot. You don't want to have to reread any questions; you want to be able to breeze through a question and know what they're going to ask before you get to the end of the question. Your brain should be so familiar with these questions that you anticipate your answer before you're finished reading.

You should try to feel the same way with the essay questions. This third time, I answered all of the essay questions for each subject (or at least outlined them). Try to complete as many of the practice essays for each subject as you possibly can. Answering these questions over and over again really is the only way for your brain to learn.

I also was really fortunate because I had another attorney who was gracious enough to act as my tutor (Jeremy, co-author of this book). He reviewed many of my essays and afterwards we went over the essays together. He was also there to offer unending moral support during those times I didn't pass the exam.

I did numerous timed essays. I think these timed essays are a really great way to prepare you for the pace of the exams. You need to be familiar with the speed you'll be expected to work at on exam day, and what better way to prepare than to actually put yourself in a similar timed situation?

I also recommend getting out in the sunshine! I would go sit by the pool and review study material from time to time just to get out of my apartment. As I mentioned before, going for a walk outside was a great way to get blood flowing and helped break up the monotony and tedium of studying hour after hour.

H. What Worked on the Bar Exam Itself?

Skipping around during essays was a TREMENDOUS help to me! I cannot stress this enough. It was something that I only decided to do on this last and final time I took the bar exam, and I fully believed it is what enabled me to pass. But be very careful to write your essays in the correct places!

My Advice Tip #3 – Briefly review the essay questions presented to you, and then choose the one you know the most about. Answer the questions in your preferred order. This will keep your brain juices flowing and you'll have more to write about (meaning more points!).

During my third attempt, I even had time to stop, go to the restroom, get a sip of water, and review my essays with time to spare. I had never felt this way in the past and I am telling you, this is the way you SHOULD feel when you have confidently answered all of the essays proficiently.

The MBE questions also became much easier on my third attempt. By this last exam, my brain had memorized so many of these questions and I could spot the issues almost instantly. My brain had memorized little variations in the questions too so I could spot exactly what the question was asking instead of being tricked.

I. Final Word

Don't be slack like I was for my first attempt. Everyone will tell you to take the bar exam seriously, and you really do have to listen to them. Start studying as soon as possible. If there is a bar prep course you can take in law school, take it. Go ahead and start preparing slowly during your last semester of law school. Once school ends and you graduate, kick everything into high gear and start studying immediately.

Postpone any big plans if possible, set your bills up on auto-pay, and tell your friends and family you will see them again in three months. Study like you've never studied before. Stick to a schedule and force yourself to repeat things over and over again. Find a tutor who is willing to review your essays or quiz you with flash cards. If study groups help you, then find a good study group.

Always remember though, if you don't pass on your first attempt, don't give up. Many, many people have failed bar exams over the years and then gone on to be successful. Just to name a few: Michelle Obama, Hillary Clinton, John F. Kennedy, Jr. and even former Associate Justice of the United States Supreme Court Benjamin N. Cardozo. You just have to pick yourself up and try again. You can't let this one exam derail what you spent years of your life building.

IV. How Ben Passed Four Bar Exams – While Working!

By Ben Klosowski, Esq.

A. Commitment and Routine

How? Commitment and routine. I looked at each bar exam as my job for about eight weeks.

Yes, the title above sounds braggadocios. But if you survived college and law school, you, too, are sufficiently intelligent and resourceful to prepare for and pass a bar exam. The difference that I discovered between some of my unsuccessful peers and me was commitment. I viewed the bar exam as my job so that I could get and keep another job -- in a law firm, eventually. I noticed that some of my peers, on the other hand, treated the bar exam as a part-time endeavor and continued to pour much of their energy into things like, ironically, the non-legal job they were in at that time. I'm not saying cheat your current employer – if you have a job – while you prepare for the bar exam; I'm just saying the bar exam must be your first love. For eight weeks, at least.

My first bar preparation and exam was in Maryland in the summer of 1998 while I was working full-time as a program manager for a systems engineering firm (a 45-minute commute each way, too), serving in the U.S. Navy Reserves once a month (sometimes two weekends a month), and my wife and I also were raising a 3-year old daughter, all with a baby boy on the way! A busy schedule, as I recall....

So, I decided after graduation from law school in the spring of 1998 – having sacrificed the preceding few years in law school – that I needed to treat the bar exam as my most important job during the eight-to-twelve weeks leading up to the exam for two reasons: first, why spend all those years and money on law school if I wasn't going to pass the bar exam; and second, I wanted to start a legal career, not to continue doing what I was doing – that was the whole point, right?

I decided that I could hold my breath and do anything for eight weeks. Why not pass the bar exam on the first try? (I have a friend who required six attempts to pass the Virginia bar. Another friend gave up after four tries. I did not want to endure that fate.)

Next, after commitment, came routine. For me, I set aside two hours every morning to practice bar exam questions and write essays. I spotted issues, made up and memorized mnemonics (I still use many of them in practice to this day!), and forced myself to actually write down answers/essays. No fooling myself with "thinking" about the answers. I would then grade my essays, literally with a red pen. If I came up with a new mnemonic or pointer, I would add it to a "Summary Sheet" that I was keeping on the side. (Keep your Summary Sheet simple. The Summary Sheet is for glancing at the evening before the bar exam, maybe the morning of. If you've recreated a "Horn Book," it will make your eyes glaze over and you might panic.

A one-page (no more than two pages) of bullet points will serve to refresh your memory and give you confidence.) Then I would go to work and take care of other responsibilities during the day. In the evening, after dinner, I would spend another hour or two working on more practice exams. I repeated the routine on Saturday and Sunday, too. After about one week, the routine became routine. It went on like that for a couple of months and finally the bar exam day arrived. The only thing I glanced over the morning of the exam was my Summary Sheet.

There are many courses, test preparation materials, and suggestions for getting us to the bar exam, so I won't delve into those, but I found that the "muscle memory" of practicing tests and writing out answers every day served me well on the day of the bar exam. This is because I was on automatic pilot - 90% of the answers jumped out at me despite being nervous, and the other 10% of the questions that were more difficult or unclear, I confidently reasoned my way through. I was confident, or calm I guess, because I knew I had nailed the bulk of the questions and essays quickly and efficiently thereby creating some breathing room for myself for the harder questions.

B. No Resting on My Laurels

I was admitted to the Maryland bar on June 24, 1999. But I didn't rest on my laurels. I wanted admission to the D.C. bar due in part to the geography and in part to the type of practice I wanted to have. Rumor at the time had it that the D.C. bar was "easy." (That's what everybody said, anyway.) Ignore such rumors. That's like kids in school talking about Old Man Smith's 5th period algebra exam – live by those rumors, die by them. So, I jumped in feet first and practiced intensely for the few weeks preceding the D.C. bar. (Notice I say, "practice" not "study" – we studied in law school. The bar exam isn't really about learning or "studying" new law; it's about practicing exams.) I did, in fact, find the D.C. bar relatively easy, not because of the content but probably because I took it on the heels of the Maryland bar and the law was fresh in my mind and because I again had committed to it with a practical practice routine. I was admitted to the D.C. bar in November 2000, first try.

This brings me to an important observation. Bar exams are artificial in that they are testing us to recall myriad laws in an absurdly compressed amount of time. If anyone practiced law under bar exam conditions, that lawyer would probably be sued for malpractice. However, bar exam preparation did instill "issue spotting" skills in me that I still use to help me begin taking apart client problems. In other words, the rote issue-spotting tool that I developed during bar preparation helps me focus to this day. Clients are paying us lawyers for our time so an efficient start can't be beat. But as an old law partner told me when a client demanded an answer immediately, "Tell him that we're on the 16th floor and there is no drive through service here!"

Turning back to my bar exam adventures, an old Navy buddy-now lawyer and I had exchanged Christmas greetings in 1999. My friend asked me to consider joining his firm in South Carolina because they needed "patent attorneys." I had the technical background to become federally registered as a patent attorney, but that would mean taking not one but two more bar exams!

Well, I interviewed with a different South Carolina intellectual property law firm in the spring of 2000, was offered a position, and joined that firm in July 2000. As expected, this meant preparing for and taking the patent bar in order to be admitted to practice before the United States Patent and Trademark Office. Beyond that, looming large on the horizon, was the South Carolina bar. Well, one thing at a time....

C. Oh, Those Squinty Looks!

There I was, Naval Officer, engineering program manager, now junior associate in a patent boutique firm. All that leadership and program management expertise, law school theory, and bar exam experience? Of some help, but knowing the law and applying it on clients' behalf?

Those are kinda different things in the real world. So, much of the work that the firm was giving to me in the beginning was light boilerplate stuff, or I was combing through piles of discovery documents looking for smoking guns – not quite the stuff of bar exam essays. In the meantime, though the firm was saying "bill bill bill," one of the partners fortunately pulled me aside and said, "Do what you can billing-wise but focus on the patent bar." Hmm. Sounded like my old mantra – commitment to the job of passing the bar exam.

So, for six weeks, while at work, if I had nothing urgent to do, I'd close the door and practice patent bar exams. I even came in a couple of hours late for a few weeks. I figured that someone would say something if I was really off-base, and yes, I got a few squinty looks from partners and associates alike, but I hung on to that partner's words to focus on the patent bar exam. That partner also said that in the long run no one would care about a few months of light billing from me (since I didn't have much practical billable experience anyway!); that they'd be happier down the road if I passed the patent bar. I did. The October 2000 patent bar national pass rate was less than 40%. What made the difference, I believe, was when I decided that the firm was paying me to become a patent attorney; that the patent bar was my temporary, primary job.

Another associate who had been hired a few months before me was a star in our firm – he had had practical experience as a patent examiner before becoming an attorney. His billing was terrific, and he was making the firm some money! Problem was, he didn't pass the patent bar with me in October 2000. He didn't pass it again six months later. A few months after that, the firm cut him loose. I eventually was selected for partnership. I think I made the right choice to focus on the patent bar.

One more thing. Right after the patent bar, I had to turn around and study for the South Carolina bar. Commitment and routine to the rescue again. I endured a few (less squinty) looks for a few weeks and passed the South Carolina bar on the first try and was admitted in November 2001. I then turned my full attention to serving my clients, and I was offered partnership about six years later.

I've been in practice for nearly twenty years now. I don't expect to have to sit for another bar exam. However, if I ever do, I will fully embrace Bar Exam preparation once again – I will make it my job, develop a routine – build muscle memory, and hold my breath for eight weeks!

Good luck!

V. A Not So Brief (But Useful!) History of John's Bar Exam Experiences

By John M. Rappold, Esq.

A. How Could This Happen to Me?

After failing the South Carolina Bar three times, I was about to give up. Nothing in my life, at least academically, had ever been so frustrating. I attended the Charleston School of Law and graduated with a respectable "B" average. I was even able to do so without exerting much more effort than I had in college, while attending the College of Charleston. I also heard that many of my classmates, who I used to study with and who, on occasion, would come to me for help with law school finals, also passed the Bar. As such, I told myself (and truly believed) that the Bar was unlikely to give me much trouble. As long as I put in the time and stayed focused, I would be walking out of that exam room with an air of confidence and an audacious smile. However, this was not my fate.

After graduating from law school in December, 2014, I decided to take the July, 2015 Bar, rather than the February, 2015 Bar. This decision was primarily prompted by a number of family matters requiring my attention, but was also made to ensure that I would pass the Bar on my first try. With seven whole months available to me now, I could wrap up any remaining familial concerns by April, still have plenty of time to swoop in and out of this bastard test, and never look back. I wasn't going to rush with only two months of preparation, only to be back in July anyway, like a lot of those suckers. I was going to buckle down and be overly prepared, with at least three months to do so.

I began with what most of my classmates and most law school graduates do, deciding whether to enroll in a Barbri® or Kaplan® Bar prep course. I had heard that Barbri® was "better," though more expensive. So, my sights were set on Barbri®. However, as is my nature, I phoned both companies a number of times to get the price down. They actually got into a bit of a bidding war, to my surprise, in order to secure me as their student. I won't digress much further, but do recommend that all students try this, as I was able to secure my Barbri® Bar prep class for about 60 percent of their listed price.

Before I knew it, I was going to the Barbri® class and spending much of my time outside of class doing what they told me to do, following their study plan. Though I put in roughly six hours per day, as opposed to the eight to ten they recommended, I felt pretty good (at least as prepared as one can sanely feel) about taking the Bar by the end of July. It was a three-day exam, consisting of two, six-hour days of essay testing and a third, six-hour day of the multiple-choice Multistate Bar Exam. I would be lying to you if I said I felt confident that I had passed the Bar when I walked out of that testing room. However, because I knew most of the answers to the questions asked and the substantive law required to answer them, I did feel my odds were…favorable. As it turned out, I did quite well on the Multistate Bar Exam, scoring a 125. This was the exact, minimum score that was required on the SC Bar, in order to be allowed to fail one essay section. Welp, I failed two… and by only a few points each. While this was frustrating, it was also encouraging. Call me a "glass is half-full" kinda guy, but failing by only a few measly points was better than being way off the mark. So, no problem here. "I'll get it next time." Right?...WRONG.

Fortunately (in my mind), Barbri® allowed any student who had taken their class but was unsuccessful on the Bar to take advantage of the same resources up until the immediately following Bar. So, after a sigh of resignation and anguish, I began going through the motions again, watching Barbri® lectures online, completing practice essays, doing practice multiple-choice questions to stay fresh on those, etc. It sucked… But I was sure that going through all of this again, after coming so close to passing on my first attempt, would surely result in a passing score this time around. I must know what I'm doing, or at least be going about this thing largely in the right

way, to have come so close.
Right?...WRONG AGAIN!

By the end of February (the time of my second Bar Exam) I felt I had picked up any and all loose pieces of the law that I may have missed before and was more prepared than anyone had ever been for any Bar...EVER! Perhaps... overly prepared. At the hotel I booked in Columbia, SC, the day before the Bar were full of countless flashcards, sample essays, and several outlines covering the same areas of law, some self-created and others from peers. As dusk came around, I was feeling pretty good and was ready to relax for a few hours before a solid night's sleep. I mean, I had done much more to prepare for this Bar than the first one, and had studied as much as one can. So, I'll be good...right? I hate to do this again, but...WRONG. I ran into a serious problem that night. I could not sleep a wink. My brain was spinning with everything I had studied over the past several weeks and especially the voluminous amount of material I had brought along and reviewed that day. I literally laid in bed from about 11pm until about 4am without any success in getting to sleep. So, I said, "#%*& it! I'll just get up, continue studying, and make sure that this unfortunate mishap doesn't screw things up for me today." This was a bad idea. Obviously, I felt horrible during the first day of the Bar. That night, I wasn't able to get more than 20 minutes of review in before falling asleep with a Civil Procedure outline strewn across my chest.

My results showed that I had failed two-thirds of the essays on BOTH DAYS! I was already pissed by what had happened before I got my results, but this made it official. Even so, every section I failed was not up to snuff by less than 10 points. I felt that I had actually put too much time and energy into this Bar, so much so that I was getting tunnel vision and letting it consume me.

For my third attempt, I did my best to keep myself busy with other tasks. I began working as a law clerk at a personal injury firm in North Charleston, SC. It provided me with a great deal of practical experience and the pay, though not substantial, took a bit of the "this could be the end of the world" edge off the Bar. This time, I felt that if I just did what I had to prepare the first time, PLUS get some sleep during the nights of the Bar, I would pass. I had the whole firm rooting for me and my boss even helped me with my essay writing.

You are probably sick of hearing about my relentless trying and failing fight with the Bar and want me to get on to the good stuff. What allowed me to pass? The next few sentences are arguably the most important in this chapter. In preparation for my third time taking the SC Bar, I studied how I had the first time when I very nearly passed. I knew the substantive law better than ever before and was able to retrieve it more readily. I felt calm, collected, and, yes, was able to sleep decently well the nights leading up to and during the Bar. Alas, I failed again.

"WHAT HAPPENED?," you ask? Yes, by this time I was able to score about a 150 on the MBE but, like my first go around, I failed two out of six essay sections by just a few points each. So, the approach I believed had to work, did not work. No matter how close to the goal I came, I still had not passed: my approach failed. If I was ever going to pass this thing, something had to change, dramatically. Now… ON TO THE GOOD STUFF!

B. The Good Stuff

For my fourth attempt at passing the SC Bar, I discarded most of my earlier Bar prep materials and took a new approach.

The third time I took the SC Bar was the last time they administered the awful three-day format, before converting to the two-day Uniform Bar Exam format. In light of this change, I thought it would be prudent to take a second Bar prep class, geared toward success on this new format. As Barbri® had not worked for me in the past, and Kaplan® was cheaper, I decided to go with Kaplan®. While I am glad that I did, it was much like Barbri®. This time, however, I didn't follow it so closely. I allowed it to familiarize me with the new (at least new to me) Uniform Bar Exam format, but did not allow it to carve out my study schedule. Of course, much (if not most) of Kaplan®'s teachings were great, and I did prefer their less-produced, less-cheesy presentation, when compared to Barbri®. However, this was not my first rodeo and I had seen it all before.

When I began preparing for the Uniform Bar Exam, I knew three things:

1) I did not need help on the Multistate Bar Exam (doing as many practice questions as you can is most effective and, in my opinion, is the best and only way to study for it);

2) I needed to find a way to effectively answer essay questions without getting bogged down in details or peripheral matters, which steals away precious time and also precious points.

3) I needed to make sure that I addressed essay questions clearly and methodically.

Interestingly, even at this point, I couldn't be entirely sure whether I was coming up short because I was actually missing the thrust of the question, or because I wasn't effectively/clearly/logically/lawyerly communicating my essentially-correct answer. Yes, I know we are all taught in law school to spell out our analysis, as if we were explaining it to a child or our grandmother. "A, in that B. B, in that C. C, in that D"… The stress of the Bar can be overwhelming and make anyone forget their "training" and rush from B to D. Was that my issue? Or was I simply addressing minor (and wrong) issues instead of the major issue? At that time, a lot of my previous Bar experience seemed a blur to me, so there was no point in trying to decipher exactly what made my answers inadequate. Today was a new day. This was a new (fourth) chance. This was a fresh start with a new Bar. Right?...RIGHT!

C. What Made It Happen/The Time It Worked/Feeling Like Rudy

First: I committed to doing 20-25 multiple-choice questions every day. I took comfort in the fact that, as long as I did 20-25 multiple-choice questions per-day (tops), I would have the entire second day, and half the Bar Exam, in the bag.

Second: Early in my preparation, I leisurely read thought the comprehensive Kaplan® outlines once. This gave me more context than I needed and made me feel like a bit of a "know it all" by the time I moved on to shorter outlines. Then, I selected the best outlines I had for each subject, and jettisoned the rest of the crap I used on the previous Bars. By "best" I mean the outlines that meshed well with Kaplan®'s comprehensive outlines, focused on the typically litigated/major issues, and ultimately made me feel the most confident to answer an essay question on the subject. So, I separated these outlines from the others, stuck with them, and never looked back. Frequently, these were the shortest outlines, like Kaplan®'s attack outlines, or another 10-15 page outline depending on the subject, but NEVER more than 20 pages. You simply do not need and will have a hard time internalizing more information than this when considering how rapidly you'll have to whip it out on the Bar. Keep in mind I am talking about subjects, like Wills, and not sections, like Wills, Trusts, and Estates. Having two outlines for each subject made me feel more secure and confident that I was not missing something (at least nothing big). In contrast, I knew that reading the same words, in the exact same order, over and over again from a single outline on a subject, my brain would eventually read the words without absorbing them. I would use these outlines to internalize the law by reviewing at least a section's worth of them every day.

Third: I watched Kaplan® lecture videos. Some would say that watching the Kaplan® lectures was not the most effective use of my time, and I might agree. However, it was nice (and I might say beneficial) to take a break, in a way, from the intense attack outline studying/practice essay writing. As with much in life, diversification is key and can actually make studying easier on your brain by keeping it interested and engaged, rather than trying to force it to be. However, I say this with caution. Too much diversification can be just that, too much. Figure out the two or three things that work best for you. If you're not sure, go with what makes you feel the most confident and willing to take on a practice essay after you're done with it. Throw everything else away! Actually, just keep it out of sight and mind, in case you need to look something up it might contain.

Fourth: I wrote practice essays. After I had spent a week or two reviewing pretty much what I already knew, aside from a few and far between "ah…I did not know that" moments, I immediately started doing practice essays. Not as many as I could get my hands on, necessarily, but enough to keep me busy for a couple of hours after reading through my two chosen, and now "two and only," outlines for each subject. I did this once a day, every day, for the thirty days leading up to the Bar, no more than two or three subjects in any one day. I did the subjects together that would be tested together, like Wills, Trusts, and Estates. Remember, this was my FOURTH time studying essentially the same material. It is okay if you're still learning the substantive law by the time you start doing practice essays. Please do start exposing yourself to them more than thirty days before the exam. Just get a good base going in your brain for each subject that you can hopefully call on to give you some confidence. And, if you're like me, the ones you miss will end up being the ones that stick, so stride on.

D. The Big Picture

If I had to say what caused me to fail the Bar three times, or what enabled me to finally conquer it in the end, the answer would be the same: 1) Practice, 2) Practice, and 3) Practice. It goes without saying, but learning the substantive law is a requirement to pass any state's Bar Exam. Memorization, though not the key, is important, and one of many keys required to unlock the complex, multi-deadlock door to admission. However, I believe learning and memorizing the substantive law to be only about 20% of the fight. What grants you entry is practice. Practice allows you to learn how to put down into your own clear effective words what you have spent so much time and energy learning from the beginning. But don't reserve practice for the home stretch, just a few days before the Bar. Instead, practice early and often. This was something I goofed up on at least my first attempt, and probably my second.

Practice multiple-choice and essay questions under timed conditions to make sure you are managing your time well. Practice to probe whether you have insufficient knowledge of black-letter law. If you do lack knowledge, go back to the two outlines you've chosen to represent that area of the law and try again. Peeking at your outlines during practice essay questions is okay early in your study, but you won't be able to manage your time properly if you still have to late in your preparation, and you certainly won't be allowed to peek at your outlines during the exam. Make the practice experience a realistic experience.

Practice to make sure that you are answering the call of each and every question. It is easy to allow issues that initially jump off the page at you to cloud your mind and distract you from what the question is really asking.

Practice to make sure that your answers address and discuss a substantial amount of the same issues that the sample answers do. Your answers and the sample answers do not have to match, and rarely do. But make sure that you don't check it off the list when the sample answer really elaborates on an issue and you barely manage to mention that issue in passing. The point is to address the issues that will earn you the most points, while leaving peripheral, smaller point-grabs for time you might have left over. If time runs short, just address the peripheral issues in a few words. This will enable the grader to give you a couple more points if you need them. Your discussion of the peripheral issues might never be read if you earn enough points to pass that essay by spending your time and words where you should, on the big-point issues.

Finally, practice to give yourself confidence and calm. No matter how secure you may feel from studying the hell out of your outlines and doing a practice essay here and there, everything changes when you walk into that room on Exam Day. The "Oh $#%^, I should have done more practice essays" feeling might hit you if you don't practice. Don't do that to yourself! It's hard to get going on them and easy to call it "good" after doing a handful on each subject. But for as much material you have to study for each section being tested, the actual questions asked typically only account for and relate to about one-fourth to one-third of that material. I can't even count the number of times I went back to my hotel room after a day of essay testing and went through my notecards or outlines in search of an answer I was unsure about, only to repeatedly say to myself, "Wow, that wasn't on the Bar...Nope, neither was any of this...I can't believe they didn't ask anything about [insert huge and 'typically tested' area of the law here].” It sucks that you have to study “everything” when this is true, but completing dozens of practice essays enables you to see several different approaches the test writers might take in assessing your knowledge. Even when I felt comfortable and was, in fact, very knowledgeable in an area of the law, I would find practice essays really helping me demonstrate that. Don’t let a lack of experience with practice essays prevent you from recognizing the context in which a law or set of laws may be addressed and really sticking it to those graders. There is nothing worse than walking out of an essay exam and overhearing someone talking about an area you know inside and out but did not discuss because you failed to recognize its applicability to the fact pattern. I have been there and it takes time to forgive yourself for it.

E. My Final Note: The Bar Exam Is Not Hard

I understand that I may seem crazy saying it, after how damn “hard” it was for me. But please, hear me out.... When I say that the Bar is not hard, I mean, it's not *that* hard. If you've graduated from law school, no matter what law school you attended and no matter if you had an A or a C average, I am confident that you can pass this thing. To touch on something I mentioned earlier, I can't count the number of my fellow law school graduates, who routinely came to me for help in law school, who passed the bar well before I did. I wasn't a straight-A student...but these were straight-C students! At first, I couldn't make sense of it. I could not believe it. How could this be? Luck? No. While there are times you may get lucky on the Bar exam, this is no True or False test. My point is...don't let yourself make this into something more than it is: a bunch of softball law school essays, all crammed into one long, exhausting endurance race. The challenge is not the difficulty of the questions, or even the amount of substantive law to which it pertains. It's keeping your cool, trusting yourself, and managing your time. It's like completing a bunch of law school essays, in the classes you got As to Cs on (hopefully), and only having to explain yourself enough to achieve a D on them. How hard can that be?

VI. Jeremy's Final Word of Encouragement

Such a diversity of experiences reveals a few key points, and many helpful details. Peter stresses discerning what is most important, and maintaining the discipline to grasp it each day. Sabrina emphasizes focus, excluding life's distractions and postponing your bar exam if you cannot. Ben presents commitment and routine as his keys to succeeding on the bar exam, showing that it is possible to prepare even while working. John's dogged determination to pass the bar exam taught him the importance of practicing and the destructive futility of cramming.

The details matter too. Creating outlines of excruciating complexity, or flash cards for that matter, do not offer a primary or universal method for passing the bar exam. **Practice**, for a few hours before and after work, for example, and early in your preparation, appears **essential**. Timed practice under realistic testing conditions builds the mind and body (and hands and butt) to tackle each question with vigor and to go the distance during two or three days of examination. And it helps to pit bar preparation companies against each other, so you can get the lowest price possible.

We see what does not work. Underestimating the bar exam means that you, too, will become an expert at retaking the bar exam. Studying, to the exclusion of practicing, does not train you to write bar exam essays or to answer multiple-choice questions.

I am most inspired by my co-authors who had to commit to retaking the bar exam after failing. Overcoming the mental anguish, self-doubt, and dejection of missing the mark by a little or by a lot, to climb that mountain again – and to **triumph** – should inspire and encourage you, Dear Reader. John's and Sabrina's perseverance shows me that they have the Right Stuff to be attorneys, too, because we will all face setbacks and defeats in our careers. It comes with the territory. Helping our clients as zealous advocates means that we put our "all" into our cases. When we lose, it hurts bad. But just like John and Sabrina, we have to pick ourselves up and Get Back On That Horse, because our clients need our help. That is why the phones keep ringing, and the e-mail messages keep coming. (Ben and Peter, taking multiple bar exams, well that's just nuts – who does that?) (Well I did that, too. Perhaps *I am* nuts. Hahahahaha!)

We hope these diverse tales inspire and encourage you as you prepare for your bar exam. If you need a day-by-day bar preparation calendar and concrete guidance on how to address essay questions, practical tests, and multiple-choice questions, please check out my book, "Pass the Bar Exam with Dr. Stipkala's Proven Method," available in hard copy and e-book. If you have feedback, questions, or comments, we want to hear from you. Kindly e-mail us at DrStipkala@gmail.com, or do a Google® internet search for us and reach us at our law practices. And we want to hear your victory speech, Counselor!

Bonus Material:

Issue Spotting and Essay Writing Techniques

By

Jeremy M. Stipkala, Ph.D., J.D.

To You, Dear Reader, Who Have Mastered All We Have Said, Yet Still Need to Conquer the Bar Exam!

Table of Contents

I. Introduction

Welcome, Dear Reader! Some of you have slogged through the previous two books, and perceive your emerging, empowering enlightenment overcoming the edgy anxiousness caused by your unproven or heretofore inadequate bar exam ability. Others of you, knowing your weaknesses, have turned straight to this book, eagerly seeking the kernel of wisdom that will propel you over the hurdle and into the Promised Land of Lawyerdom, *because essay questions suck*.

What brings *me* here? I have just finished another season of mentoring attorney candidates to pass the bar exam. I watched with great satisfaction another batch of future attorneys turn their considerable legal knowledge into an organized, accessible body of information, marshalled by a disciplined approach to each question on the bar exam. And I have no idea if they all will pass. Now begins the longest months of the year, not just by number of days, but longest due to the uncertainty of waiting for bar exam results to emerge at the end of October. A slight frustration that **maybe I could have done more** to help my friends compels me to write more, with this book targeting the hardest part of the bar exam.

A. Why People Fail the Bar Exam

What follows builds on what I said in the *Method* book about the need for structure upon which to build the answer. *See* pages 47-48, above.

In my estimation, attorney candidates who fail by a lot of points struggle with addressing the question and giving the answer the bar examiners seek.

Imagine you are a bar examiner grading the same essay written by hundreds of attorney candidates. Most candidates have written more or less the same essay. Most hit the main issue, and many note several of the same minor issues. The grading process becomes a little bit of a blur. You see the same words arranged more or less in the same order, and you bestow points accordingly. Point, point, point, pass. Next: point, point, point, pass. Next: Ah, what the hell, pass. You can see, as soon as you open the essay, whether this attorney candidate adequately addressed the essay question. And so it goes.

Then you open an essay that Does Not Look Like The Others. This essay is shorter. Or it goes off on some tangent. If it has an earnest tone, you look back at the essay question itself, to see if the question fairly raises that tangential issue. No, not really, it doesn't. You assign points where you can, where the essay obliquely hints at the issues actually raised by the question. Then you assess: Even though this essay missed the point of the question, does this candidate deserve to be an attorney? Your eye takes in the full, meager arc of the essay, and you conclude: Sadly, no, not yet; almost. Fail. Next.

Attorney candidates who fail by just a few points, in comparison, do not give enough of an answer to get enough of the points. "Defendant is liable because all of the elements of negligence are met in this case." That could be a perfectly correct answer to an essay question. However, it is too short, and cannot possibly receive the same number of points as the essay that correctly explores the issues of proximate causation and contributory negligence fairly raised in the fact pattern. You see, essay questions *are not about getting the right answer.* (Multiple-choice questions do that.) Essay questions focus on whether the attorney candidate **can think like a lawyer.** And, to do that, you must follow the instructions of your middle school math teacher: **Show Your Work.**

How do you get good at issue spotting? Practice! How do you get good at writing long, thorough essays that gather many points? Practice! *How* do you practice? Read on!

B. Why – and How – People Pass the Bar Exam

People who pass the bar exam write essays that **get it**. They spot the main issues, address them succinctly and correctly, and move on. They correctly state the rule of law, or a close approximation thereto, and then apply the most relevant facts to the elements of that rule. (It is my view that your perfect articulation of the rule of law is less important than your *analysis* of the rule. Put another way, the bar examiner grading your essay asks, "Did this attorney candidate apply the facts to the rule *as written?*") To pass, the attorney candidate must spot the issue with some degree of precision, state a decently accurate and relevant rule of law, and then coherently apply the facts to the rule and conclude whether each element of the rule is present. In other words, the attorney candidate follows the All Elements Rule. *See* section on All Elements Rule starting on page 64, above. More points are gotten when the attorney candidate also follows the All Evidence Suggestion, especially when analyzing the element(s) of the rule central to resolving the dispositive issue(s). *See* section on All Evidence Suggestion starting on page 68, above.

People who pass the bar exam also treat minor issues quickly and succinctly.

Think of this as the **extra credit** on the bar exam. When you are all finished tackling the dispositive issue, write a sentence or two (or three) mentioning that you spotted other minor issues. That may get you an extra point (or three!). Consider using a sentence like, "There is no [minor issue] in this case, because there is no evidence of [whatever facts would raise the minor issue]." Or, "[Minor issue] arises in this case, because of [evidence relevant to minor issue in fact pattern]. However, [minor issue] would not change the outcome of [the dispositive issue]." *See* the Model Answer starting on page 254 below to examine how I deal with minor issues in a sentence or two.

It all starts with issue spotting. Spot the wrong issue, and you write one of those tangential essays that causes the bar examiner to purse her lips and shake her head "no." Spot the *right* issue, and the bar examiner's eyes glaze over in mild boredom as she confers a passing score to yet another attorney candidate. You can do it! Read on to learn how!

II. Issue Spotting

A. Issue Spotting When You Spot Too Many Issues

Ideally, your well-prepared mind reading the fact pattern will bubble forth with issues as the facts conform with the rules of law bursting from your brain. In some cases, the facts of the question will conform to facts of previous cases of which you are aware. "This fact pattern sounds like that case where Fourth Amendment rights were violated," you might say to yourself. But you must discipline that bubbling spring of issues to grasp the most-important issues, or even the *one* issue, upon which the question turns.

The issue usually can be stated as a "whether" clause. Broadly, "The issue in this case is whether the elements of the governing rule of law are met." Well, please don't write that on every essay on the bar exam. Instead write "The issue is whether . . . ," and finish that thought with something relevant that addresses the question.

Know this: **The question provides the best clue of the issue.** Read the question carefully, every word, before you read the fact pattern. Constitutional law issues will contain words like "constitutional," "unconstitutional," "interstate commerce," and other buzzwords that you have seen before, for example. But watch for "assuming" clauses: "Assuming the statute is constitutional," signals that the question wants you to *set aside* the constitutional law question. Or, the "assuming" clause wants you to set aside one constitutional law question to address a different constitutional law question. That is why you must read *every word* of the question before you do *anything* else.

Multiple questions mean DO NOT ANSWER THE SAME QUESTION TWICE. I will give you an example, building on the foregoing. Suppose the first question says, "1. Construct an argument that the statute is unconstitutional." The second question says, "2. Assuming the statute is constitutional, does the state agency have to enforce the statute?" A talented attorney candidate will answer the first question with a wonderful exposition of the interstate commerce clause, say, and conclude, "Therefore, the statute is unconstitutional because Congress did not have the power to regulate this matter under the interstate commerce clause." Perfect. Full points for the first question. But the *inattentive* will answer the second question, "Because the statute is unconstitutional under the interstate commerce clause, the state agency does not have to enforce the statute."

Uh oh! That answer, Dear Reader, clearly ignores the "assuming" clause. In the second question, the Bar Examiners seek your knowledge in a different area of the law. Our poor attorney candidate will receive no points for the second question, because she did not address the power of the federal government to compel state agencies to action, which the second question begs for treatment. Also, there may be less-obvious ways (other than an "assuming" clause) by which questions direct you to address different areas of the law. Your biggest clue is that *there is more than one question.* Once you tackle the issue(s) of the first question, you must unshackle your brain from that question to address the remaining questions with a clear mind. Know this: **Do not give the same answer to two different questions.**

Another Useful Tidbit: **Glance at the substance of all questions when you are orienting yourself.** The reason to do this is simple: The bar examiners may be seeking a full elucidation of your knowledge in one area of the law. On the South Carolina bar exam, there were three questions following a fact pattern. In each of the three questions, the facts were slightly different. "Assume [some fact] is true for this question. Did Buyer reasonably rely on Clerk's statements?" Those three questions gave me the clue that the bar examiners were exploring (a) apparent agency authority, (b) inherent agency authority, and (c) express agency authority. Ah! What relief to see that clue from the structure of the questions! (In my reading of the questions, at least one of them poorly conjured the desired source of agency power.) My answers addressed each of the three sources of agency power, and I gave the bar examiners exactly what they wanted.

Now it may come to pass that the several questions are unrelated. Do not force a pattern that is not there. For an example, take a look at the Example Essay Question below. (Hint: the three questions Are Not Related.)

Know this: **Issue spotting skills come from practice.** Just like it takes two thousand practice multiple choice questions to get ready for the Multistate Bar Exam (*see* what worked for Sabrina, on page 162, above), it takes many practice essay questions to get ready for the Multistate Essay Exam. If your issue spotting skills really suck, do this: Add an hour each day to your exam preparation dedicated solely to issue spotting. In that hour, read every essay question you can get your hands on. Write the issue for each one, in a "whether" clause. Abbreviate "The issue in this case is whether" as just: "Wr." Then write a detailed issue. (**Write** it out! Writing more effectively trains your brain than just mumbling it to yourself.) Next, immediately read the model answer for that question. Did you spot the correct issue? Did you come close? Can you add to your written issue a word or a concept? Go ahead and write that additional word or concept now, to input it into your brain. (Later on, as January becomes February or June becomes July, add Rule Articulation to this issue spotting exercise. Can you spot the right issue, and then write a good rule, too?)

B. Issue Spotting When You Have No Clue

Be ready for an essay question for which you have no clue. It happened to me on my last bar exam. *See* pages 70-73, above. On Exam Day, if you simply cannot discern the issue or remember the rule, you can still pass the bar exam. Let me encourage you: You can still show the bar examiners that you deserve to be an attorney. In fact, this could be your moment to shine. Let me give you some insight into the greatest essay you will write on your bar exam. It will be the greatest because you will have to bring every ounce of your Inner Attorney to bear. And when your Inner

Attorney emerges, the bar examiners grading your essay will know: An **Attorney** Wrote Here.

Importantly, **if you can write the issue, you can write the rule.** It is so true. Your statement of the issue appears in the articulation of the rule. Using the issue as the foundation for the rule allows you to move forward even if you do not know all of the elements of the rule. "The issue here is whether the defendant can support an entrapment defense." Yes, I wrote that in my bar exam essay without knowing the elements of an entrapment defense.

First, do not panic. Take a deep breath to oxygenate the brain. Next, read the question carefully again. Can you turn the question into a statement? Look at this question: "1. Construct an argument that the statute is unconstitutional." If your mind simply goes blank, write the following in your AIRAC outline: "Answer: This statute is unconstitutional because_____." Yes, I know that this restatement of the question appears so very simple. But it orients the mind on the right path – the panic-stricken, clueless mind. (I pray you do not find yourself there on Exam Day.) Now consider the second question: "2. Assuming the statute is constitutional, does the state agency have to enforce the statute?" Write this in your AIRAC outline: "Issue: Whether the state agency has to enforce the statute." Well. That was easy. But that leads you to the harder task of articulating the rule of law that governs: "Rule: A statute is unconstitutional [under the _______ clause] when Congress lacks the power to regulate the subject matter of the statute." And: "Rule: A state agency must enforce a federal statute when ______."

Next, review the question and what you have written for inspiration. On the constitutionality question, try to come up with reasons why a statute has been held unconstitutional. For the state agency question, can you develop reasons why a state agency might act, or could refuse to act, because of a federal law? This is where the intensity of your preparation comes to bear. Did you hear anything in bar prep lecture? Did you read anything in your outlines? Are these questions similar to any of the practice essays you have done? (This is why we do **many practice essays**, Dear Reader! *Nothing else* will train your mind more effectively.) Force your mind to explore those places it has traveled recently in preparing for the bar exam, with the goal of jogging a memory of anything relevant and useful.

Read the fact pattern, or read it again. Perhaps reviewing the facts will jog a memory of another essay, a relevant rule, something. If no memory surfaces, go for *inspiration*. What should the issue be? What should the rule of law be? You are Emperor for a day, and you get to make up a rule to govern this fact pattern. What shall it be, Your Highness?

If nothing comes to mind, and you have tried everything a couple of times, *move on to the next question*. Get points where you can get them. While you are busy with another essay, a rule just might pop into your head. Jot it down, and continue with the essay at hand. Then come back to the problem essay at the end of the exam. Just be very careful to write your essays in the correct places! And remember, you do not need to pass every single essay!

I offer you the foregoing techniques to keep your mind from going completely blank in the face of a question for which you initially have no clue. In the bar exam, keep your mind moving, even inching forward, so it does not leave you stranded on the thought that you are in the middle of the bar exam and your panicky mind just went blank.

So, if you encounter some area of the law for which you forget or do not know the rule of law, do the following:

Breathe.
Turn the question into a statement.
Write the issue – then write the rule.
Review the issue, the question, the fact pattern for inspiration.
Move on to the next question and come back.
Write your essays in the correct places!

III. Rule Articulation

A. Creating a Rule When You Know Part of It

So there you are on the bar exam, writing your last essay. Only part of the rule comes to mind. Or you have nearly finished writing your essay, and more elements pop into your head. What do you do?

You can go with what you have. That may be sufficient in some cases, and you will merely pass with a lower score. Guess what? A pass is a pass! Or you can rack your brain for more elements to fill up the time you have left with point-getting effort, just in case the points already earned do not add up to a passing score. I strongly encourage you, Dear Reader, to write your butt off until time is called. I am aware of an attorney candidate who scored 265 on the Uniform Bar Exam. Passing required 266 points in her state. Guess what she had to do? That's right: retake the *entire Bar Exam!* So push yourself to get more points right until "time" is called.

Let's deal with the easy situation first. You have nearly finished your essay, and more elements pop into your head. If you are typing your essay, well, no duh, insert the additional elements into the rule and then into your analysis. If you are hand-writing your essay, do your best to legibly squeeze in the additional elements and analysis in the appropriate places. (*See* page 125 above, where I encourage you to write double spaced.)

Now for the harder situation. You have half the rule written down, but you do not have the most-relevant, dispositive parts of the rule surfacing in your mind. Write your essay with what you have, and leave room for the additional elements when they come to mind. Apply the facts to each element that you have, and leave room. Then, re-read the question, the facts, and what you have written, and see if something useful completes your thoughts already expressed. If memory does not enlighten you, consider the Rule Creation ideas in the next section.

B. Creating a Rule from Scratch

Okay, it is your last essay. You have skipped this one, because nothing came to mind. You wrote your butt off for the other essays, and confirmed that you were writing your answer in the right booklet/place. Thirty minutes, or more realistically twenty minutes, remain. It's glory time! Take a deep breath, remind yourself that you don't have to pass all of the essays to pass the bar exam, and roll up your sleeves to do a little legislating from the bar exam bench.

You have a fact pattern and a number of questions. You know that the first question carries the most weight. Now it is time to Make Up A Rule Of Law And Analyze It Just Like A Lawyer.

Rule-making on the fly, when all other options are exhausted, might touch upon the following topics:

Party
State of Mind
Acts
Instrumentalities

Consequences
Time Limits
Burdens of Proof

Let us explore each topic.

1. Party

Who are the parties to the suit? Can you identify the party upon whom the rule of law will rest? Who is the defendant? Is the plaintiff in a protected class, such as a child, or a subsequent buyer without notice?

2. State of Mind

If there is a crime involved, what is the mens rea required? Should a person be held liable under the law if the person acted negligently, grossly negligently, recklessly, in the heat of the moment, intentionally or willfully, or with premeditation and malice aforethought? If the matter does not relate to an evil (or negligent) mind, did the party have notice? What kind of notice – actual, apparent, or record notice? For example, was a deed recorded but a party did not bother to look for any recorded deeds?

3. Acts

What did the party do or fail to do? Did they have a duty to act, or to refrain from acting in a certain way?

4. Instrumentalities

Does the rule you are creating relate to instrumentalities or tools? For example, a person cannot violate a speed limit law without a motor vehicle. (Or can they?) What if someone runs a stop sign on a bicycle? One cannot violate the law against discharging a firearm within city limits if they do not have a firearm, right? Cars, bicycles, and firearms are instrumentalities that can appear in the elements of a rule of law.

5. Consequences

If someone violates your rule of law, what is the consequence? Are they guilty (criminal) or liable (civil)? Of what?

6. Time Limits

Is there a statute of limitations? Is there a grandfather clause? For example, you cannot violate a seatbelt law if your (ancient) car lawfully has no seatbelts because it was manufactured so long ago.

7. Burdens of Proof

Does the plaintiff need a preponderance of the evidence to win? Or is the burden heavier? Clear and convincing evidence, perhaps because there is a presumption against the plaintiff? Beyond a reasonable doubt? Or are you facing an appeal? Findings of fact below may be reversed for clear error, or the no-reasonable-jury standard. Conclusions of law turn on *de novo* review, in many rules of law. If the lower court had discretion in a matter, look for abuse of discretion for reversal.

With the foregoing topics in mind, can you cobble together a rule? Let's try one on for size. Suppose the fact pattern relates to a driver getting a speeding ticket. Can you imagine the party (defendant driver), state of mind (notice based on posted speed limit), acts (driving in excess of speed limit), instrumentalities (motor vehicle), and consequences (guilty of speeding)? There is probably a statute of limitations, and the burden of proof is likely beyond a reasonable doubt, because traffic laws carry criminal penalties usually. Can that lead you to articulate a rule of law, such as, for example, "A defendant is guilty of speeding if the defendant was driving a motor vehicle in excess of a posted speed limit?" "Prosecution for a speed limit violation must be brought within two years of the alleged violation, and proven beyond a reasonable doubt?" (I have no idea if those rules are correct in your jurisdiction, Dear Reader.)

Once your issue is spotted and a rule of law composed, the essay should write itself. The hard, mental part is over (mostly). All you need to do is plug in the facts to the elements, following the All Elements Rule and All Elements Suggestion, and reach a conclusion. (Make sure you answer the question!) And voilá! You are done with that essay!

Practice, Dear Reader, once in a while Making Up A Rule From Scratch. When you are practicing your issue spotting, and feel that you have nailed the issue, but do not recall the rule governing that issue, attempt to concoct a rule before looking it up. Your legislative skills developed this way may save your bacon on an essay or two on Exam Day.

Indeed, you may find that sometimes you remember the rule cold. Every word, every element of the governing rule of law pours forth from that photograph in your brain that you visualize right there during the bar exam. But sometimes, you will construct a rule, and the line between memory and legislating-on-the-spot will blur. Afterwards, you will ask yourself, “Did I remember that rule cold? Or did I make it up?” The answer, Dear Reader, is that it doesn’t matter. Sure, you write the rule a little funny. Maybe you lose a point or two. But as you write your analysis, examining each element in turn, you reveal that you deserve to be an attorney because you have thoroughly analyzed the rule as written. And you pass.

Let me emphasize. You must **practice writing essays**, and that starts with practicing issue spotting and rule articulation. And you must practice for **two months** before the bar exam. No person could walk in off the street, armed with the foregoing, and pass a bar exam, making up all the rules of law along the way. *That is true even if the person off the street graduated from law school!* I offer the foregoing only to help you get a few extra points on your bar exam once you are fully prepared and have nearly finished the essay portion of the bar exam itself. Or the foregoing may help jumpstart your studying and practice-essay writing. Do not rely on these ideas as a secret shortcut for passing the bar exam. That would be like reading this about running: "Left, right, left, right." And then going to run a marathon.

IV. Essay Organization and Writing

A. Allocating Time

If there are multiple questions, know that the first question is usually the most important, and the last question is usually the least important. That means the first question gets the most points! There may be more than one issue, such as notice to shareholders and the business judgment rule, in the earliest question, while there is only one issue, such as *ultra vires* action, in the last question. Know this: **give more time and attention to the first question than to the last question (usually).**

How do you do that? When you open your essay examination, look immediately for the question or questions toward the end of the fact pattern. See how many questions there are. If there are three questions, and you have thirty minutes, then simple math tells you to spend ten minutes on each question. However, that allocation does not account for two things: First, some of your time will be spent simply digesting the fact pattern. You will spend more time doing that for the first question than for any other question. Second, you already expect the first question to offer the greatest number of points. So if there are three questions, with the first question being the most important, you might allot twelve minutes to the first question, ten minutes to the second, and eight minutes to the third. If there are four parts, allocate ten minutes to the first question, seven minutes to the second, seven minutes to the third, and six minutes to the fourth.

B. AIRAC, Your Friend

Now it is time to organize your answer to the first question. I offer you the AIRAC system. *See* page 48 above.

(I will pause while you re-read about AIRAC on page 48. Come back here to page 230 when you are ready.)

Write on your scratch paper or on your screen AIRAC, down the page like this:

A
I
R
A
C

Read the question carefully, and then the fact pattern again. Now determine the issue that decides the case. Are there two issues? For example, one issue could be whether the defendant was negligent, and another issue could be whether the defendant's actions actually caused the injury complained of. Or, the sole dispositive issue could be the causation element. Do you see how two issues could collapse into a single issue? Importantly, if you spot more than one issue, it could be that there is only one main or dispositive issue. Economy of time and effort may require you to collapse multiple (perceived) issues into one. In this hypothetical, you might write the following in your outline:

A
I: Wr negligent -> causation.
R: Duty, breach, causation, injury.
Causation: but for; proximate/foreseeable.

A
C

In your analysis, you might write: "Here, the defendant clearly had a duty to drive reasonably, breached that duty by running the red light, and the plaintiff driver clearly suffered injuries to his car and his arm in the accident. [Notice the brief treatment of the cause of action - negligence.] So this case turns on whether the oil slick in the intersection breaks the chain of causation to absolve the defendant from liability." And then you go on to wax lawyerly about causation. Once you have mentioned those elements of the cause of action (negligence) that are beyond controversy – duty, breach, and damages – you need not spend more time on them. But you should address them! An essay about causation that fails to mention all of the elements of negligence appears incomplete.

C. Multiple Issue Essays

What if there truly are two issues? For example, let us suppose in our little traffic accident that the victim was busy texting while driving. Hopefully you will see that the one issue is the negligence of the defendant driver (who is being sued), and his negligence turns on causation. And I hope you can see the second issue, which is the contributory negligence of the plaintiff driver (who was texting). Construct an "AIRAC" structure for each issue. Do not conflate the two into one, at least because one driver's negligence does not impact the other's. (Contributory negligence may bar recovery, though, in some jurisdictions).

Be careful to structure your treatments of the two issues so that you do not make your essay unnecessarily complicated. For example, the defendant driver could countersue the plaintiff driver for negligence. If the question does not seek that claim, don't make it. (Example: "On what theory could plaintiff driver sue defendant driver?" That question fairly raises defendant driver's negligence and plaintiff driver's contributory negligence, but not the counterclaim.) If you have extra time, only then would you consider adding the counterclaim. But it is not the point of the question.

Do you see from the above examples two distinct circumstances? In the example with the oil slick, the sole dispositive issue was causation. Causation is but an element of the rule of negligence. I submit that the oil slick example really has only one dispositive issue. In contrast, the second example had the plaintiff driver texting. Thus, there are two issues, both potentially dispositive. First, there is the negligence of the defendant driver, and that issue turns on the causation element (he still had an oil slick to skid through). If he was not negligent, he wins. Thus, that's your first dispositive issue. Second, there is the contributory negligence of the texting driver-plaintiff. If he is contributorily negligent, his recovery can be limited or barred. That's your second dispositive issue. The point: **construct an AIRAC structure for each dispositive issue**, collapsing perceived multiple issues into one or fewer issues where possible, but not conflating distinct issues.

V. An Example Essay Question

A. The Fact Pattern and Questions

Okay, let's take a look at an example essay question to practice our issue spotting and essay writing skills. The facts come from a real-life situation of which I am aware. In the words of that great thinker and commentator, Dave Barry, "I Am Not Making This Up." (He's also *really funny*.) Ready?

> Mom and Dad married many years ago in West Dakota and domiciled there during their marriage. They had Kid and enjoyed a happy time for a number of years. Eventually, though, Mom and Dad divorced due to Dad's frequent and lengthy deployments with the military. In the divorce decree, Mom was awarded primary custody of Kid, and Dad was ordered to pay child support to Mom until Kid turned eighteen years of age. Kid turned eighteen five years ago.

Dad served in the military thirty years before retiring two years ago. Dad is now domiciled in East Carolina. Upon reviewing his retirement pay information last year, he discovered that $400 a month is being garnished from his pension for "back child support plus interest." The office of the attorney general of West Dakota has placed the garnishment on Dad's federal military pension alleging $80,000 in back child support plus interest.

Dad's pay stubs and financial records show that child support had been properly deducted from his military pay for every year since the divorce, and the alleged arrearage in missed child support payments is a mistake. Dad has obtained a court order from a West Dakota state court ordering the West Dakota attorney general's office to audit Dad's financial records to determine whether the garnishment is lawful. However, the West Dakota attorney general's office asserts the following positions:

(A) The West Dakota state court order is insufficient; only a federal court order can compel the West Dakota attorney general's office in this matter.

(B) The West Dakota attorney general's office will perform an audit only for a West Dakota resident who can show sixty days of permanent residency in West Dakota.

Dad does not want to establish residency in West Dakota to qualify for the audit. Instead, Dad comes to you seeking help.

Question 1: Construct an argument that the attorney general's position requiring West Dakota residency is unconstitutional.

Question 2: On what jurisdictional basis could you bring an action in Federal court to compel the West Dakota attorney general's office to perform an audit?

Question 3: Does Dad have a cause of action against Mom to recover improperly garnished pension money?

(I will pause for a moment while you freak out. Is this a Family Law question? Constitutional Law question? Civil Procedure question? It is a real-life question, and it is complicated! I have simplified it somewhat; but the attorney general's office really took those positions. Dad actually established residency in "West Dakota" before obtaining the state court order, and still did not get his audit. And, lest you think that "West Dakota" is a fictionalized name for some small state in fly-over country that you'll never visit, this actually happened in A Really Big State That Ought To Know Better.) (This question exemplifies why society needs you as an attorney! Stuff like this really happens.)

B. Orient Yourself to the Questions

First thing to do is to read the questions quickly. The purpose of your first read of the questions is to orient yourself to the task at hand. "How many questions do I need to address?" "What is/are the general area(s) of the law I must use?" If you read the fact pattern first, you will get bogged down in the details. And you will have opened the Family Law box in your brain as soon as you saw Mom, Dad, and Kid in the fact pattern. "Best Interest Child," you will have scribbled on your scratch paper, to no purpose as we shall see. Instead, read Question 1 quickly. "Unconstitutional." The Con Law box opens in your brain, and that is A Good Thing. Now read Question 2 quickly. We're bringing an action in federal court. Open the civil procedure box. Is there a federal question? Is there another source of jurisdiction? Those thoughts will surface when you read Question 2. Read the third question. Dad versus Mom trying to get his money back. Sounds like a family law/civil procedure/contracts question.

Now divide your time. The happy news is that in less than thirty minutes from now, this question will be history. Knowing that the first question usually carries the most points, and the last question usually carries the least number of points, we are going to allocate our time as follows: Question 1 will get twelve minutes (a few of which we will burn just orienting ourselves to the fact pattern); Question 2 will get ten minutes, and Question 3 will get the remaining eight minutes. A glance at the time reveals that a couple minutes already have passed.

C. Tackle Question 1

Focus now on the first question. Read every word. "Question 1: Construct an argument that the attorney general's position requiring West Dakota residency is unconstitutional." We already know what the answer will be. "The attorney general's position requiring West Dakota residency for an audit is unconstitutional because ." Set up your outline, on scratch paper if you are writing, and on your screen, like so:

A
I
R
A
C.

If you like, type in the beginning of your answer to your outline, if your outline will form your essay. There is no need to do this on your scratch paper, of course.

Now rack your brain for a suitable constitutional doctrine. On its face, it just does not seem fair that the attorney general can garnish Dad's retirement payments, but Dad cannot get the attorney general to double check that garnishment unless Dad moves to West Dakota. That implicates the Equal Protection Clause of the Fourteenth Amendment, because the attorney general is creating classifications of people based on residency. So write the issue in your outline (I assume you are typing for the outline below):

A The attorney general's position requiring West Dakota residency for an audit is unconstitutional because

I The issue is whether the attorney general's position violates the Equal Protection Clause of the 14th Amendment of the US Constitution.

R
A
C

Now it is time to write some rules in your outline. The Fourteenth Amendment provides that "No State shall . . . deny to any person within its jurisdiction the equal protection of the laws." Great! But there is more. The attorney general's classification of people by residency might be lawful if it rationally relates to a legitimate state interest. Or, you can argue that as applied, the attorney general's residency requirement falls disproportionately on men, since in a divorce, men are more likely to be the breadwinners subject to wage garnishment and need this kind of audit. The classification here is not based on classic suspect distinctions such as race or national origin, however. So write those rules.

"A state's action based on residency violates the Equal Protection Clause if it bears no rational relationship to a legitimate government interest." And: "A state's action based on gender violates the Equal Protection Clause if it is not substantially related to an important government interest." Interesting question: Which rule do you pick? Do you analyze both? If you have time, handle both. And do not forget the task at hand: you are constructing an argument that the residency requirement is unconstitutional. You are *not* deciding *whether* it is unconstitutional. (Notice I am putting two rules in one AIRAC structure – they are alternatives for the same issue of unconstitutionality, easily treated together.)

Now write your analysis for each rule. Tick off each element. Is West Dakota a state? Is the attorney general's action a state action? Is Dad a person within the jurisdiction of West Dakota? Now dive into the equal protection aspect based on the residency classification. Here, the state wants to ensure that residents obtain child support from non-resident ex-spouses. Yet there is no greater burden (I would argue) on the state providing an audit to a resident than to a non-resident. West Dakota can require either a resident or non-resident to appear in a West Dakota government office to conduct the audit.

What about gender discrimination? Apply the All Elements Rule and analyze. To the extent the residency requirement disproportionately falls on men, the state has an interest in ensuring women receive the full measure of child support due. But whether a man lives in West Dakota bears no substantial relationship to ensuring that women have the financial support due them.

Now write your conclusion: "West Dakota, a state subject to the 14th Amendment, has denied Dad equal protection of its laws on the basis of Dad's residency in another state." Go back and complete your first sentence of your essay, so your grand answer does not dangle after the "because" you already wrote. And you are done with Question 1!

Whatever you do, do NOT go over your allotted time for Question 1! You MUST attend to Questions 2 and 3 with sufficient time to give them proper treatment! If you have run out of time for answering Question 1, leave some space to write more later and move on to Question 2.

D. Tackle Question 2

Turning now to Question 2, note that you have ten minutes. Now read the question carefully, every word: "Question 2: On what jurisdictional basis could you bring an action in Federal court to compel the West Dakota attorney general's office to perform an audit?" Okay, we are suing the attorney general in federal court. Who is the plaintiff? And why do we want to compel an audit? Now read the fact pattern carefully, knowing that we are looking for someone to be our plaintiff, and that plaintiff needs an audit.

Reading the fact pattern, we see that Dad has a problem with the attorney general garnishing his retirement pay to the tune of $80,000. "Wait a second," you might think. "Could this be a job for diversity jurisdiction?" Yes! But don't stop there, not yet. Force your mind to evaluate other possible sources of federal jurisdiction, like federal question jurisdiction. Could there be some federal question jurisdiction attaching to matters of federal military retirement pay? Could be. But nothing I learned in law school really appears on point here. Also, I recall that there is legislation on the books that protects military spouses in the event of a divorce – but that doctrine does not apply here, because the military spouse, Mom, got her due and more. I also note that state's immunity from suit comes to mind. But if that applied here, Dad would have no redress whatsoever. Also, Dad cannot sue the attorney general personally (probably), because the attorney general is acting in his official capacity: the attorney general has personal immunity so long as he acts within the scope of his office. Sooooo, the lowest-hanging fruit is diversity jurisdiction. Let's go with that.

My point is this: Do not scribble/type away on the first doctrine that pops into your head. Pause for a microsecond to ask yourself if there is a more-germane doctrine.

Now it is time to outline our answer using diversity jurisdiction. Write AIRAC down the page of your scratch paper if you are writing, and on your screen if you are typing. (Check: are you typing your answer in the right spot?) Now write the issue. Your outline might look like this:

A
I Wr Dad can sue atty gen in fed court on diversity jurisdiction.
R
A
C

Now write the rule:

A
I Wr Dad can sue atty gen in fed court on diversity jurisdiction.
R A plaintiff can sue a def in fed court if the pl and def are citizens of different states and the amount in controv is greater than $75k.
A
C

As I write that rule, I wonder if every element is precisely correct. Do they have to be citizens, or is it "residents," or does the correct rule state "domiciled in different states?" Also, is the amount in controversy element correctly stated as "at least $75k," "$75k or more," or "over $75k?" Finally, what about U.S. territories and foreign countries? I vaguely recall that the diversity jurisdiction rule does address those situations.

Here's where precision does not matter. Sure, those who recite 28 U.S.C. § 1332 precisely from memory in their essays will get the most points. But the bar exam is not testing you on the razor sharpness of your memory. The rule recited above is reasonably accurate and states all of the material elements. Significantly, it should receive enough points to pass.

At this point, I would write no more in my outline, if your outline appears on scratch paper. It is time to begin writing your essay.

If you can confidently answer the question, then write it down as your first sentence. (This is the first "A" in AIRAC.) If you cannot yet answer the question, then leave some space to write it in when you can. Write your issue and rule in full, without abbreviations, where your essay answer goes. "The issue is whether Dad can sue the attorney general in federal court on diversity jurisdiction. The diversity jurisdiction rule allows a plaintiff to sue a defendant in federal court if the plaintiff and defendant are citizens of different states, and the amount in controversy is greater than $75k."

Now write your analysis, starting with "Here" or "In this case." Address each element, naming the plaintiff, the defendant, the citizenship of each, and the amount in controversy, all while referencing the fact pattern. Following the All Elements Rule, address every element. Acknowledging the All Evidence Suggestion, use every piece of relevant evidence in the fact pattern.

Then write your answer as the first sentence of the essay, if you haven't already. Re-read the question so you can frame your answer. "Dad can bring an action in Federal court to compel the West Dakota attorney general's office to perform an audit on the basis of diversity jurisdiction." Congratulations! You have fully answered the question!

However, more points are to be gotten! First, you can flesh out the details of the action you would bring. Are you seeking an injunction, or a writ of mandamus? Second, here is where you can raise ancillary issues that show You Went To Law School. "Dad must be careful to sue the attorney general in his official capacity, as the attorney general likely has official immunity from personal suit in this case." "It appears that the immunity of West Dakota is not implicated in this case. If it were, Dad's garnishment and need for an audit could not be redressed in court." "Mom's current citizenship is not relevant here."

If you really have lots of time, you could construct an AIRAC analysis for one or more ancillary issues. For example, you might AIRAC the issue of the attorney general's personal immunity, because his goofy positions (*see* positions (A) and (B) in the fact pattern) colorably go beyond the attorney general's duty to faithfully apply the laws of the land. But make no mistake: that is a tangential issue that should not form the main thrust of your essay, especially when diversity jurisdiction begs for treatment on these facts. If you focus on the West Dakota attorney general's possible lack of personal immunity to the exclusion of the diversity jurisdictional issue, your essay will sound like a crackpot wrote it, not an attorney. (I think personal immunity remains for the attorney general here, anyway.)

When your allotted ten minutes for Question 2 expire, move on to Question 3.

E. Tackle Question 3

You have eight minutes. Read Question 3 carefully, every word. "Question 3: Does Dad have a cause of action against Mom to recover improperly garnished pension money?"

Wow! This sounds like a real snipe hunt. Could we say that Mom has been unjustly enriched? Did she commit an act of fraud to get the attorney general to garnish Dad's retirement pay in the first place? If there was no fraud, did Mom have a duty to return cash that she knew or should have known was excessive? How do we know if she should have known it was excessive?

I am going to go with unjust enrichment, because we have no evidence of Mom's bad acts, if any. The fact pattern does not reveal at all what Mom told anyone, and it is entirely possible that the garnishment is a purely administrative mistake. But Mom got money she did not deserve, and should give it back to Dad.

We begin by writing our last AIRAC outline. Having decided to go with unjust enrichment, we can write the issue, too. If you are really clever, you can type the answer, too, leaving space to insert a "no" that will flip your answer if you so choose:

A Dad has   cause of action to recover improperly garnished pension money from Mom under the doctrine of unjust enrichment. [In the space before "cause," above, write "a" or "no" depending on what you decide!]

I The issue is whether Dad can recover Mom's unjust enrichment.

R
A
C.

Now formulate a rule for unjust enrichment. Make up a rule, if you have to, using the guidance appearing on pages 222-228, above. "A plaintiff can recover from a defendant's unjust enrichment if the defendant has enjoyed an enrichment, the plaintiff has suffered a loss directly related to defendant's enrichment, and the defendant can offer no defense or justification for the enrichment."

Analyze the rule, every element, and use all of the relevant evidence you can. Write your conclusion, complete the answer that is the first sentence of your essay, and you are done. If time remains, add a sentence about there being no evidence of fraud, or anything else that comes to mind.

F. Proofread if There Is Time

If you are completely satisfied with your treatment of Question 3, and you have time left, proofread! Read your essays and fill in any blanks. Correct any spelling errors. Read for coherency. Correct any sentence fragments or gibberish. Check the All Elements Rule. Acknowledge the All Evidence Suggestion. Skim the fact pattern once again, and insert any additional evidence where possible (or necessary!) Re-read the three questions. Did you answer all three?

As the proctor calls, "Time," and your pen lifts from the page, smile, Counselor! You have finished (and passed – I hope!) the Bar Exam!

G. Model Answer

Here's the Model Answer that I wrote. It builds on what I said above, following another read through the fact pattern to glean more tidbits and points. Please keep in mind that my Model Answer should not be viewed as an authoritative treatise on the legal issues raised in the fact pattern. Instead, it should be viewed as a realistic treatment of the facts according to the law in a bar exam setting.

Imagine that you are the bar examiner grading this essay. Do the essays answer the questions? Do you discern my AIRAC organization? Do I deserve to be an attorney, or should I try again?

Question 1. The attorney general's position requiring West Dakota residency for an audit is unconstitutional because it violates the Equal Protection Clause of the 14th Amendment. The issue is whether the attorney general's position violates the Equal Protection Clause. That clause provides: "No State shall . . . deny to any person within its jurisdiction the equal protection of the laws." A state's action based on residency violates the Equal Protection Clause if it bears no rational relationship to a legitimate government interest. A state's action based on gender violates the Equal Protection Clause if it is not substantially related to an important government interest.

Here, Dad is a 'person within [West Dakota's] jurisdiction,' at least since the attorney general has power to garnish Dad's retirement pay. Further, Dad got married and divorced in West Dakota, and his ex, Mom, lives there. The attorney general is a state actor, so is subject to 14th amendment.

West Dakota has a legitimate interest in ensuring that its resident ex-spouses like Mom receive all the child support they are due. The attorney general is acting in a manner that discriminates on the basis of permanent residency. That means, in practice, permanent residents of West Dakota are treated differently, and better, than residents of other states like Dad. However, the state can require either a resident or a non-resident seeking an audit to appear at an appointed place within the state for that audit, thereby affording the state no different burden due to the residency or non-residency of the person seeking the audit. Because the sixty-day residency requirement for an audit bears no rational relationship to West Dakota's interest in obtaining child support payments from non-resident ex-spouses, the residency requirement violates the Equal Protection Clause and is unconstitutional.

The residency requirement for an audit also fails under the Equal Protection Clause for discriminating on the basis of gender without being substantially related to an important government interest. The requirement falls disproportionately on men, since men are more likely to be the breadwinners, therefore subject to garnishment, and therefore needing an audit. West Dakota has an important interest in ensuring that its women ex-spouses receive all the child support they are due. But whether a man lives in West Dakota, and denying him an audit on that basis, bear no substantial relationship to ensuring that women have the financial support due them. This is shown by the Attorney General's ability to garnish Dad's retirement pay no matter Dad's residency status. Accordingly, the attorney general's requirement for permanent residency for conducting an audit of a garnishment violates the Equal Protection Clause as it disproportionately falls on men with no substantial relationship to the important government interest.

Question 2. Dad can bring an action in Federal court to compel the West Dakota attorney general's office to perform an audit on the basis of diversity jurisdiction. The issue is whether Dad can sue the attorney general in federal court on diversity jurisdiction. The diversity jurisdiction rule allows a plaintiff to sue a defendant in federal court if the plaintiff and defendant are citizens of different states, and the amount in controversy is greater than $75k. Here, Dad is domiciled in East Carolina, and the facts suggest residence and therefore citizenship there. The state government of West Dakota, of which the attorney general's office is a part, is considered to be a citizen of West Dakota for diversity jurisdiction analysis. The attorney general alleges there is $80k in back child support and interest, meeting the $75k amount in controversy requirement. Accordingly, diversity jurisdiction allows Dad to sue the attorney general in federal court for an injunction compelling an audit.

Dad must be careful to sue the attorney general in his official capacity, as the attorney general likely has official immunity from personal suit in this case. The attorney general garnished payments acting within the attorney general's apparent authority. It appears that the state immunity of West Dakota is not implicated in this case. If it were, Dad's garnishment and need for an audit could not be redressed in court. Mom's current citizenship is not relevant here, as she would not be party to the suit between Dad and the attorney general seeking an audit. That Dad's retirement pay comes from the federal government suggests federal question jurisdiction as well, if there is a federal statute protecting such retirement pay in these circumstances.

Question 3. Dad has a cause of action to recover improperly garnished pension money from Mom under the doctrine of unjust enrichment. The issue is whether Dad can recover Mom's unjust enrichment. A plaintiff can recover from a defendant's unjust enrichment if the defendant has enjoyed an enrichment, the plaintiff has suffered a loss directly related to defendant's enrichment, and the defendant can offer no defense or justification for the enrichment. Here, Dad's retirement pay has been garnished by $400 per month for the past five years. Mom has received that garnished pay. Because that garnishment was incorrect, Mom has received payment unfairly at Dad's expense. Mom can offer no defense or justification, because the garnished money represents an amount above and beyond that to which she was entitled by the divorce. According to the evidence, Dad properly paid all child support due when it was due, as shown by his pay stubs and records. Therefore, Mom has been unjustly enriched and should pay the extra money back to Dad.

There is no evidence here that Mom committed fraud by lying to obtain the garnishment. We do not know from the fact pattern how the garnishment arose. Even if there was fraud, on top of unjust enrichment, Dad can recover only what he lost. He cannot enjoy a double recovery – that would be unjust.

VI. Final Final Final Word of Encouragement

Dear Reader, I am sending you Good Vibes. You can do this! You got this. Breathe, and practice. Get practice test materials, and build those callouses in all the right places. You earn your license to practice law in the two months leading up to the bar exam; the two or three days of the bar exam itself merely prove it.

Work on your essay skills, especially issue spotting and rule articulation. Then build out your mental endurance by writing out full essays, especially as Exam Day approaches.

When you get the Good News, do three things. Celebrate! You deserve it! Then resolve to pay it forward, and help others, including those who struggle to pass the bar exam. Finally, send me your Victory Speech! I want to hear how you did it. What worked, what did not work, and what can I do to improve the guidance found in this Great Work Of Fine Literature. Ha. I'm at DrStipkala@gmail.com.

10866038R00149

Made in the USA
Middletown, DE
14 November 2018